THE ROAD TO KILIMANJARO

From the Poorest Country in Europe to the Pinnacle of the World

SERGUEI MELNIK

ISBN: 978-1-956464-23-8

First Edition 2026

This publication is intended to provide accurate information on the subject matter covered. It is sold with the understanding that neither the author nor the publisher offers legal, investment, accounting, medical, or other professional advice. The author and publisher make no representations or warranties regarding the accuracy or completeness of the contents and expressly disclaim any implied warranties of merchantability or fitness for a particular purpose. No warranties may be extended by sales representatives or materials. Professional consultation is recommended as individual circumstances vary. Neither the author nor the publisher shall be liable for any damages, including but not limited to loss of profit, incidental, or consequential damages.

Published by BrightRay Publishing
https://brightray.com/

Table of Contents

———————•———————

First to my kids, the center of my universe:

You will not be reading the book anytime soon as you are just children now, but that is one thing that will inevitably change. One day, you will become adults, and I am sure I will not be ready for that.

So I hope when you read this note, you will still want to have a conversation with your dad, who might not be as cool or hip anymore as you remember him from childhood. I hope you will answer my phone calls, or at least call back as soon as you can because I know how much I cherish my time with you now; I can just imagine that it will be a thousand times more precious as you grow up.

Love you always and forever,
Dad

Next, to my wife Jazmina:

Jazmina inadvertently joined on this road to Kilimanjaro from the beginning in June 1994. She and my friend Igor, were with me at that restaurant when the American representative of the Moldova Florida Organization was very vividly describing someone else's experience at Kilimanjaro. From then on, I was inspired.

Little did Jazmina know that she would become my total and unconditional support in this lifetime journey.

I love you Jazmina, and thank you for creating a happy home with me and gifting to me these amazing treasures, our children.

And, of course, to my parents:

Through unimaginable difficulties you managed to raise and educate two very successful individuals, myself and my younger sister. Thank you for all of the sacrifices that you had to endure in order to give us a chance. I am so lucky to still have you around to see our successes.

Introduction

Ever since I was young, I have had incredibly vivid and mysterious dreams that ended up being quite foretelling, giving me senses of the good or bad that is to come. With this in mind, I have come to latch onto a quote from Alexander Blok's "On the Field of Kulikovo":

> ... And back to the eternal battle
> The peace is just in our dreams

This quote rolled through my head as I waited by the bar in the Citrus Club on a rainy Valentine's Day evening. My wife, Jazmina, left my side to find the washroom, so I stood by myself, gazing out a window at the streets of downtown Orlando. I could not have dreamed of COVID-19 stretching into its second year and that going out for a Valentine's dinner would finally offer a sense of normalcy, one I needed in the chaos of preparing my company, Nutriband, for a listing on the NASDAQ.

In light of world news and personal stress, Valentine's Day had slipped my mind, and though I knew I could easily find a gift for my wife, I called all over town trying to reserve a table; it seemed impossible to find a nice restaurant at the last minute. Fortunately, I remembered the Citrus Club, where I'd been a member since 1999— the Citrus Club always delivers with super classy, white-glove service and impeccable food and atmosphere. They were the only penthouse in Orlando that had a table ready for the same day, yet when we arrived, Jazmina received flowers from the staff, and we immediately felt welcomed.

As raindrops ran down the panes of glass, I weighed the words, "the peace is just in our dreams," and how back in Moldova, it was everyone's dream to study in the United States, and somehow this dream became my reality as I now live in the sunshine of Florida. How had I achieved this peace over everyone else? If this was the peace, starting a family and multiple businesses in the United States, what was my eternal battle?

My successes did not come without a price as over the years, my morality and integrity have been challenged by difficult business decisions that forced me to confront unsavory practices. At one point, I was naive enough to believe the lies of greedy men, but I can say with pride that I haven't abandoned my ideals in my work. I've built companies from the ground up and watched companies crumble under their own weight, and with all of these experiences, I have learned the importance of honest and transparent business. Eventually, I found partners and friends whom I wholeheartedly trust, knowing that our shared ideals would result in a stronger business: another dream turned into reality.

I met one of those friends, Igor Andries, in law school when I still lived in Moldova. In June of 1995, we were having a pleasant dinner with Michael, an American who was representing the Moldovan Florida organization that sent me to the US the year before as an exchange student.

My future wife, Jazmina, was also present at that dinner. During the pleasant gastronomical experience of traditional Moldovan food, Michael started telling us about Kilimanjaro and how the climbers that make it to the top are exposed to the most beautiful sunrise in the world.

Mesmerized by Michael's romanization, Igor and I made a promise to one another: whoever reached the threshold of $1 million first would arrange the hike up Mount Kilimanjaro for the both of us. It became a symbol for us, where we would climb over the obstacles of the world with hard work and determination, just as we would eventually summit Kilimanjaro and stand above the clouds looking out at the savannah and (as I had been told) the most beautiful sunrise in the world.

I reached my goal by the age of 31 in November of 2003. The night before I rang the opening bell on the American Exchange floor, I had an extraordinary dream where I was flying through the clouds. On the following day, I felt that same lightness, the joy of our work being recognized. It was a great achievement, one I wouldn't have dreamed of reaching as a child, but after I hit it, my mind pivoted to the next goal. Even though I had over $1 million in equity, I did not feel that I achieved that clean break of success to be able to climb Kilimanjaro. There is always the next project or the next deal, and soon those inspirational dreams of summiting in Tanzania fell to the wayside… But the idea stayed with me.

As of writing this, I will turn 50 in August of 2022, and my sense of accomplishment in the world of business has been satisfied. The major achievement I have left for this chapter of my life is to reach the top of Kilimanjaro. I've been involved in sports since I was seven, playing soccer and competing in judo and jiu-jitsu, and I've climbed mountains in Ecuador. My body and mind are ready, and I feel this is the time to see this through to the end.

Moving forward, what matters most in my life now is my family and giving my children the support they deserve. If I could bring them on this trip to Tanzania, I would, but they are too young. Before I step back and focus on my family, I feel I must walk the length of my life, starting from the bottom and climbing to the top of where I am today. With this mindset, I'll scale Mount Kilimanjaro.

CHAPTER 1:
Childhood in Moldova

When I looked up, two giant, blue wings beat down, forcing the air around me to swirl my hair and toss it back. The wings shadowed my face as they flapped above me. It was a blue butterfly, massive in size, flying across the sky, and just the sight of it filled me with immeasurable happiness and hope.

Dreams have played a key role in my understanding of my intuition, usually giving me deep insight into myself or problems that I am struggling with.

To eight-year-old me, this was just a dream, but I did not know that a dream about a butterfly could push me or give me the confidence to venture out into the world, making my own path. Despite its enormous size, we do not naturally have blue butterflies like this in Moldova, but the butterfly is a symbol of wealth, luck, love, and many good things to come. These were bold ideas for a young boy like me growing up behind the Iron Curtain—nothing gets through, neither in nor out.

One of the few times that something did sneak under the Iron Curtain, I remember making a prophetic wish on New Year's Day of 1981 while watching the New Year's Day concert. Usually, the Soviet TV would show these concerts at about 2 am on New Year's Day, which was pretty much the only time you would be exposed to foreign pop and rock music. I paid particular attention to beautiful women singing about Rio de Janeiro. For my nine-year-old boy mind, these women were the most beautiful phenomenon I had ever seen. I did not understand the language they were performing in; I just understood "Rio de Janeiro." This was enough for me to say to myself, "I will marry someone from Latin America." I just didn't know how I would meet someone like that while in Moldova. A couple of years ago I set myself an objective: to roam through youtube until I found that videoclip from the 1981 show. It did not take long ago and there they were, the two beautiful girls singing about Rio de Janeiro, only they were not Latin-American, the girls were not even American, they were two Dutch sisters: Aaltje and Doetje de Vries and the group was called Maywood... and they definitely had more cloth on than I as a 9 year old remembered.

Exploring the world as I have was never made to seem like a legitimate option for my future. As a child, I read the true story of a boy who dreamed of being a sailor and traveling the world. He snuck onto a cargo ship but became trapped in between containers in the hold, waiting months to emerge from the journey across the Atlantic. He started out with some luck by breaking into a container and finding food and water, but the rats soon ate what little supplies he had. Eventually, he had to catch the rats and eat them raw in order to survive—a gruesome tale, but this boy was proud of the adventure he went on. From behind the Iron Curtain, I too dreamt of adventure, but I never truly believed I could break free from the limits of Moldova and what was expected of me by my parents.

Some of the adventure of my youth was found in playing sports, but I was never allowed to take it more seriously than exercise. My parents never thought that sports could be a career or path for my future, yet they were the ones who initially encouraged me to play. I had my tonsils taken out when I was five, but after that, I would get horribly sick with a sore throat and the flu every winter. I would end up in the hospital and take a long time to recover, so my parents did what they thought would make me stronger: they had me play sports.

The more sports I played, the better my health was, and soon, I didn't have to worry about going to the hospital every year. Ever since then, I haven't stopped playing sports; they continue to fuel my competitive nature and keep my body and mind strong. My relationship with sports was left for me to deal with independently though as my parents did not think sports could advance my life in any way.

Once, I came home from a soccer game excited to find my mother. I could not stop telling her about how many goals I had scored, but her answer to me was, "Well, you're never going to be a soccer player, so don't get too excited about that." Instead, my parents were most passionate about sitting with me doing homework and reading; it was nice to bond with them while working on it together. I still explored sports, even though I was left to do it alone.

All throughout school, I played soccer and wrestled—I was even the star of the school soccer team—but my father never saw any of my games. He did not drive me to soccer practice either. I would walk by myself about three miles back and forth each way to the stadium three times a week starting at the age of 7. The only soccer club available in town was through the nearby Russian school, and I was the only child from the Moldovan school training at the time. Surprisingly,

I was made to feel that I was different at every point, even though I looked exactly like them and spoke Russian with no accent (courtesy of 3 years at a Russian Daycare before going to school). At every turn, they would try to pick a fight with me and make me feel unwelcome. Stubbornly, I kept training in that club for four years; nothing was going to separate me from my passion. It was after I turned 11, I decided it was time to learn how to fight, so I joined the judo club that was luckily based at the Moldovan School. Later playing soccer for my high school, I would regularly face off against my former teammates from that Russian club: nobody would dare to pick a fight with me ever again.

In my most exciting high school soccer game, we played against our rival village on their field, so we had no supporters in our stands, only enemies jeering at us and hoping for our loss. Eventually, I was able to score the first goal—this is one of the most beautiful goals I had ever scored. I received a long pass from a right defender and without letting the ball drop to the ground, slammed it from about 35 yards straight under the upright, sending the ball under the crossbar and past the goalkeeper and leaving the local village dead silent as our team pulled ahead. Ten minutes later, I scored again, and by the end of the game, we had won 2:1.

Even though we had won, there was no one around to celebrate our win as the rival village left their field, which was a familiar feeling to me. I had led our team to a win, but the win was less of a victory to enjoy—my family was not present in the crowd, and there was no one cheering for me.

This was always frustrating to see as my parents would give my sister, Alina, plenty of support in her activities. My mother and father would make the time to attend my sister's dance recitals, but when it came to my sports, they did not seem to care what I was doing, except for one wrestling match out of my entire wrestling career.

There was a surprisingly large turnout for the city judo championship, and this included my sister and parents in the crowd. My father had been a champion freestyle wrestler when he was in college, but even still, he was not present at any of my matches before this, including when I made it to the district finals and the national championship three years in a row.

The city wide scope of the judo championship meant I was wrestling against my peers—we had trained and wrestled together for years. I won matches on the way to the finals, but in my final match, I was up against Sasha Curos, who was in a heavier weight class than me. Sasha and I had wrestled many times before, but I had never once been able to beat him as it was hard to get the edge over him. In the finals, with my family watching from the crowd, I risked it all as I fought Sasha; I pulled off a difficult maneuver and before I knew it... Sasha tapped out—I had won.

This match against Sasha was a turning point in my life where, even if I didn't realize it until later, the victory would give me a confidence boost in my own strength.

It reminds me of what would eventually become one of my favorite movies, *Mr. Destiny* (1990), where Jim Belushi's character gets to live an alternate reality of his life where he didn't strike out in his state high school baseball game. I had that too: the one moment of victory in front of my parents caused a domino effect of life events that would bring me to where I am today.

This was the first time I had seen my father be truly proud of me, and because of that, I wish he had spent more time at these sporting events. The fact it stands out as a singular memory has inspired me to try to attend as many of my own children's sporting events as possible. I feel awful even if I only miss a practice, something with such low stakes, but I know how it feels when you don't have someone supporting you along the way. It fills my heart with joy when my son, even at practices, makes a good play or scores a goal. Right away, he is looking for me in the crowd to check if I saw it.

I do not put the blame on my father's ambivalence to my wrestling and soccer activities as I know he was always busy with his own career, especially when he was vice mayor of the city. At one point, his political career overlapped with my athletics and almost had detrimental effects for the both of us. Very importantly, these events drew us much closer together than we ever were.

My father was on track to be promoted from vice mayor to the Second Secretary of the Communist Party, but he often did not see eye to eye with the First Secretary of the Communist Party in the district, Mircea Snegur, who demanded more respect than he deserved.

I remember it very clearly — during my summer vacation, my mother came home very stressed and incredibly flustered, telling me to clean around the house as she held back tears. When I asked what was wrong, she broke down, crying and telling me that dad had been arrested. The police chief, Mr. Railian, a lackey of Snegur, had ordered my father's arrest, and a case was opened to investigate any wrongdoing. My father was handcuffed, paraded through town to garner humiliation, and then released home the same day, restricted from leaving the district while the case was investigated. For over a year, my father couldn't find a job as every time he would apply for work, he was denied, which he later found out were instructions coming from local communist leadership. For that year, we relied on my mother to support us all. Eventually, my dad was hired as a VP for the president of the Kalininsk Bread Factory, Mr. Zaharia, a former school peer of my dad. My father warned him of the directive from above not to hire him, but Mr. Zaharia said that he was not afraid of those Communist Party clowns.

The police had no case though and failed to prove anything in their investigation; the people they tried to say gave bribes to my father refused to testify because they did not even know who my father was. A journalist from the Soviet Moldova newspaper (*Sovetskaya Moldavia*) wrote an article after the official resolution on the case was issued.

After all these years, I remember the name of the article, "Honor of a Uniform," (*Cesti Mundira*) as I can still see my mom and dad reading it with tears of joy and redemption in their eyes. The article went into meticulous details of the case, reporting on people being held in cells to give false testimonies against my dad. All of the Snegur lackeys involved were punished as a result of the article—the chief of police, Railean, was removed and stripped of his grade, and the District Attorney was reassigned to a lower position in a different town—but one very important and inconvenient detail to the Communist Party was left out: Snegur's name, the evil behind the whole ordeal. By the time the case was resolved, Snegur was promoted to the highest echelons of the Communist Party of Soviet Moldova, and he moved to the capital city of Chisinau.

Unfortunately, the damage was done, and my father's political career was killed as Mircea Snegur would eventually go on to become the first president of Moldova in 1991 when I was a freshman in law school. It was a hard time for my family, and my father slowly tried to build up his political career again, except my fighting spirit would make life even harder for us.

Put on by the school, discotheques were popular spots for young people to meet up and dance, and all grades would mix and mingle on the dance floor. I went with my girlfriend at the time and found that a senior, Anatol Paduca, kept being disrespectful to her. In the heat of the moment, I invited him to the gym locker room where I threw a few fateful punches at him, even though I was only a sophomore, and busted up his lip in three or four places.

The repercussions of the fight would come fast, but we tried to make amends—my parents were from the same village as Anatol's parents and at one time close friends, so I was brought to Anatol's apartment that same night and had to apologize for the incident. Our parents exchanged pleasantries, and it seemed as if the apologies had been accepted... until the very next school day.

Anatol's mother went to the school principal and insisted that I be suspended from school and punished. I, being a judo champion who got into a fight, would face severe repercussions. I was suspended for two weeks, and it was the first time anyone at the school had been suspended for a fight. It felt like political retribution against my father, who was trying to revive his career in public service. At the time, it all felt like the worst moment of my life—my father coming out of this two-year ordeal suddenly having to deal with his son being suspended for fighting made me miserable. The suspension and the fight not only tarnished my own records and followed me into my college career, changing my life forever, but it also cemented my father's political career from ever coming back.

At the time, I felt it was for the worse, but it was all as the universe intended. Not long after the fight incident, my father received an official apology for the false charges from the Communist Party officials and the city, and he was appointed president of the largest construction company in town. Anatol's father happened to work at that company as the main engineer, although he had been hoping to reach the position of president.

I think Anatol and his family should have read Shakespeare before engaging in a vengeful act: "Heat not a furnace for your foe so hot that it do singe yourself." Anatol's dad was fired shortly after my dad took over the company. At one point, I asked my dad why he fired the guy. My dad's short answer was: "What did you think I should do with someone who tried to hurt you? Besides, he was a lousy engineer."

I learned much about being a moral man from my father, and his lessons have stayed with me for the length of my life as I conduct business and raise my children. For as much as I regret not having my parents supporting me more as a child, I always felt love from my grandparents.

In the summer of 1980 our family was reunited with our relatives from Ufa, Russia, fatherland of my Grandpa where he had a son in 1943, before he was sent to Moldova in 1944 and before he met and married my Grandma. The next time I would see my family from Ufa, my uncle and my cousins would be in summer 2018 during the Soccer World Cup that was hosted by Russia. We lost all of our contacts with the Ufa relatives after my Grandparents passed away, but I was able to find my cousin through the Russian Social Network Odnoclassniki.ru, he had on his page the same picture that I had in my family album, the entire family happily reunited in the beautiful Town Park of Edinet, Moldova in the summer of 1980.

Family reunion in Ufa, 38 years later

Grandpa's childhood home in the village of Engalasego approximately 40 km (25 miles) from Ufa.

*My precious tourists are admiring the beautiful City of Ufa
from the balcony of our hotel.*

*The last game that we saw live in the stadium during
the 2018 World Cup 2018: Argentina vs Nigeria.*

First years of judo. I am the third one from the let in the upper row. To my right is Sasa Curos, victory over Sasa in the final of City Judo Championship was in my opinion one of the decisive moments that would shape my fate in the years to come.

My Grandpa (Tatunica), hero of the Great Patriotic War. When Germany invaded the USSR on June 24th, 1941, Grandpa was in military school and he was just 20 years old. He was assigned to a Scouting Unit and was gravely wounded later in 1941 on his last mission. After his recovery, Grandpa was sent to Moldova in the fall of 1944, after Moldova was liberated from the fascists.

My mother's father, "Tatunia," was a war hero having fought in World War II and the Winter War in Finland when he was a graduate of military school. Back then, going to military school was the only thing guaranteeing that you would not die of hunger. My mother doesn't know much about my grandfather's family because they perished in the famine. My grandfather became a rock in my eyes, and this unshakeable image of him was heightened by all of the war scars that covered his body. "Mamunica," my grandmother, outlived my grandfather by 11 years, and I was lucky to have my wife meet them before they passed on.

Jazmina met them for the first time in June of 1995 when I returned from an overseas school engagement. I remembered we gathered all of my big family, including my mom's two brothers with their families, at my grandparent's farmhouse. If only someone would have told me that was the last time we would gather like that. My sadness in losing them is still overwhelming at times, but we were lucky we already had camcorders at that time and can now relive that moment whenever we want on the screen.

My mother's parents held a special place in my heart as my sister and I would spend the summers with them on their farm for a month or two at a time. Their land had all sorts of fruits: cherries, blackberries, raspberries, apples, plums— not to mention the animals. Thinking back on the farm, it only reminds me how lucky I was to have such a positive childhood. I can even directly point to one of the happiest moments of my life on the farm.

One morning, when I was just around 11 years old, I woke up and had such a light feeling in my chest, almost as if I could start floating and fly away. The late morning sunlight that filtered through the large walnut tree's leaves outside and shone through the window was striking. All of the doors and windows were open, so the drapes fluttered as the air moved through the house; I could hear the voices of my grandparents as they were setting up the breakfast table for everyone outside.

Breakfasts were always special as my grandmother would go and pick fresh strawberries from the garden and mix them with homemade sour cream, courtesy of our cow, Joana. Fresh eggs, laid overnight by the chickens, would be retrieved from the barn and served alongside freshly baked bread pulled right from the oven. We would all congregate under the huge pear tree, sipping hot black tea as the clean and pure country air swirled around us, accompanied by the noise of the chickens, ducks, and wild doves in the trees.

It truly is one of the happiest memories I have, and it only reaffirms how lucky I was to have a solid childhood before going out into the world, eventually moving on from behind the Iron Curtain. I had many trials and tribulations ahead of me, but I always had that core memory of the farmhouse to keep my heart pure and ready for everything that would come.

CHAPTER 2:
University and the USA

————————•————————

Living under communist rule, I had no natural inclination towards an education in business or capitalism as generally, life behind the Iron Curtain meant being in "survival mode." You were taught to think that everything is decided for you and that the state will handle all of the decisions you would otherwise need to make for yourself. You would be given a job, you would have a salary, and you would set on a predetermined path, but this illusion began to shatter as the Soviet Union began to weaken and disintegrate.

I was in the generation most affected by these changes. The future was uncertain but suddenly more open to our dreams and opportunities.

I could dream of going to college and pursuing opportunities, but the consequences of my fight at the school dance meant that my hopeful reality had hit a snag. Punching Anatol and the suspension stained my school record, affecting my chance for the silver medal award. Having a medal was necessary to avoid the hassle of three tough entry exams into law school. If I had the medal, I would have been enrolled into the university automatically when I aced the first exam. Unfortunately, after the next two exams, my testing scores were too low for the average of three entering exams. I felt like a complete and utter failure with two Bs when I needed all As.

I watched as all of my friends went off to universities, starting their careers, while I was left behind, seething at Anatol and his family along with those who had tried to destroy my dad. I was psychologically devastated as I worked for a year in a mechanic shop, working on cars and trucks while my friends sat in classes and started their careers. I was further frustrated when my friends would come by the mechanic shop to visit—me covered in oil while they were clean from the capital city where they studied.

I had trouble accepting this, and my survival mode kicked in: I would have to accept this loss, not getting into university, but I would never wallow in defeat and accept failure as an option. I found no peace inside until the next spring, when I began to prepare for my law school entry exams again, giving myself purpose and drive. Failure was not an option anymore.

After a year of working in the mechanic shop and studying everything for the law school entry exams, I took the test, and finally, I was admitted into university. There were just 75 freshmen students accepted to law school at the Moldovan State University (the only law program in the country). I was number 67 on the list after my entrance exams and the rest of my extra curriculum and sports records were taken into consideration.

Part of the serendipity of my late admittance was meeting my friend Igor, who was a year younger than I and who I would later plan to climb Kilimanjaro with once we made $1 million dollars. It all goes back to my *Mr. Destiny* moment; defeating Sasha in that match gave me the confidence, but also the arrogance, to take on a senior at the discotheque and set my life on its current path. My time working at the mechanic's and watching my classmates move on was humbling and grew a sense of determination in me. This youthful drive to explore life more fully, including capitalism and making money, came at a strange time in my life but also Moldova's development.

While in university, the Soviet Union was in its death throes, and during this transition period, a small number of people became wealthy, a concept I was still coming to terms with having grown up relatively poor. At school, I was exposed to rich kids whose parents had privatized a factory or stole from the crumbling Soviet coffers—I saw people driving new exotic cars, eating in restaurants every day, and living lavish lifestyles. This was only a lifestyle for very few though. As Moldova seceded from the Soviet Union in 1991, many suffered from the confusion and disarray.

Moldova struggled to form its newfound republic under Mircea Snegur, and its cities faced chaos as food was limited and bandits roamed the streets due to the lack of a government-funded police force. What few police there were could often be found covering for the bandits. It makes my skin crawl to this day thinking of those who lost their lives in our dangerous streets and received no justice. I knew the work I wanted to do should distance myself from the growing corruption in Moldova. While I was able to study at university, this was no easy task for my roommates and I either.

With Moldova's secession, food became scarce when we needed it the most, and college students like us could wait in bread lines for hours and still receive nothing. Every fall, we could normally work at collective farms for two or three weeks out of an academic year, a state-sponsored program where young Moldovans could go and help with farming produce. We were paid in food and very little cash. The whole idea that food would not be an issue to find during this time was very comforting. Plus, the collective farm work was one of the greatest bonding experiences a young lad could ever experience, with great parties after work in the local village discos; our time out often led to scuffles as we would try to pick up local girls, but it was all in good fun.

One night as we bided our time until we would go off to the collective farm, I was starving alongside my four roommates in our small dormitory, where we either had no access to water or the bathrooms leaked toilet water into the halls. We were supposed to be shipped to Southern Moldova to collect grapes the very next day, where food would not be the problem anymore as we could expect three meals a day.

All five of us scrounged what food we could find, and together, we had one chicken and some potatoes. Igor Andries went to the kitchen to warm up the already cooked chicken and fry the potatoes while the other four roommates: Dorin Covali, Sahsa Parfeni, Sergiu Branza and I played cards anticipating a savory feast with our stomachs growling because we hadn't eaten all day. When Igor stepped out of the kitchen into the corridor, holding the pan of chicken and potatoes, proud of this dish he'd prepared for us all out of such meager ingredients—and then the handle snapped on the pan. The chicken and potatoes fell into the toilet water that had flooded the halls, and all our hungry eyes filled with abject horror.

As we picked up the potatoes that had not been soiled, an upperclassman passed by in the hall, and looking down at our chicken, he smirked at us, adding, "Bon appetít."

I couldn't help but think how the year before we were eating affordable food and getting by, but now this newfound democracy was not being handled with the care it needed. In fact, it was being abused by those in power as war in Transnistria was brewing due to separatists and Russian influence.

In 1992, Moldova was preparing to engage Russian-supported forces in Transnistria, so recruiters and war mongers came to our university to rally students for the war effort. They were talented propagandists who played on our hurt national dignity, appealing to a "now or never" urgency of their own creation. Many of us were swayed by their words, and we were herded onto a bus and swept away towards the renegade republic of Gagauzia.

As I arrived at the south city of Kaul, where the center for enlisting into the national guard was settled, I quickly realized what a mistake I was making, the strongest catalyst being that my girlfriend was visiting from Orhei where she was studying to be a teacher. Weighing the protection of national pride against a fun weekend with my girlfriend at my dorm, the choice was obvious, so I got off the bus and headed back to Chisinau.

Come Monday, I was shocked to find my mother waiting for me at the university, visibly relieved when she saw me showing up for my classes. The recruiters had been filming us getting on the buses, and it had been broadcast on TV, where my mother had seen me amongst all the other students heading off to war. I appreciated my mother's concern, but I think I knew deep down that fighting battles with guns and tanks would not be my path in life.

This picture was taken at the Dormitory #11 of the State University of Moldova during my studies at the University Law School. Costea Morar is the first one on the left, my high school classmate, he graduated from the Medical University and became a renowned surgeon and went back to make his life in our native town Edinet, in the North of Moldova, I am next with a winter hat, Oleg Alexa (to my left), my best friend and my roommate Igor Andries (next to last from the right) and Igor's step brother Vasile Andries, that was history major at the Moldova State University later on becoming a PhD in History and professor at the same University.

Alexandru Ilco (first from left) graduated from Medical University and become a prosperous physician in România and to my left is Dorin Coval, with his hidden genius.

In my third year of law school, I had a fortuitous dream about hearing a speech coming from the other side of a massive wall, though I could not see who or what was talking. I knew it was in a foreign language, and I began to climb over this wall only for the language to slowly become recognizable to me. By the time I had reached the other side of the wall, I knew exactly what was being said. At the time, I was focused on learning French because I had previously taken it in school; it would have been an easy course to take. It was one thing to study a foreign language at the time, but it was another thing to actually utilize it—Igor would be the one to change all of that for me.

I didn't plan on studying English, but it was a very fashionable language to learn as private classes were opening all over town. Igor was relentless, pestering me to join his English class, so when the French class was closed due to a lack of students, I finally agreed to attend English class with him. He told me not to worry, even though I had never studied English in my entire life, yet I somehow got into the first-level advanced English course... and I had no idea what was going on. I quickly set my mind to learn enough English to make the course worthwhile.

By the end of the year though, a contest was held for a studying abroad program sponsored by George Soros. I had progressed to where I felt more comfortable with English and tried to convince Igor that we should compete in the contest, but Igor was adamant we were going to fail and needed to study more. I decided I was going to take a chance and applied to the contest anyway.

After going through the application process and testing, my English skills were just good enough that I passed, and had Igor applied, he might have made it as well. Instead, I had earned the scholarship to attend the University of Hungary for the summer, and with the help of my father, I was able to get my first passport and head off to Budapest to learn more about political economics at the Central European University, formerly known as Karl Max University.

In Hungary, I met a few Americans, and they piqued my interest in studying in the United States—if I could study abroad in Hungary, why not the United States?

Again, an invisible hand led me to where I needed to be in my fourth year of law school in Moldova, and again, my friend Igor missed out, though this time wasn't entirely his fault.

For the law program, part of our curriculum was going to the hospital every Monday to evaluate and observe psychiatric patients: what caused psychological problems, how those affected are not criminally responsible, and why some need to be cared for in the facilities. My friends and I decided to stay on the university campus instead of going to the hospital, but Igor never made it to school that day as his car broke down on his way back from his hometown. While on the campus, I was mindlessly exploring the special programs offices, where I found an American woman holding interviews for a study abroad program in the United States, so I decided to go through the interview process.

My English at this point was good, but I would be participating in an interview with native English speakers for the program. Still, I found myself making it all of the way to the end of the interviews. By fate, luck, or skill, I was given the chance to go to the United States to study at the University of Central Florida for my senior year between 1994 and 1995. Mr. Sedletsky, the dean from our law department, accommodated my exam schedule so I could catch up when I got back from the US in May of 1995.

When I arrived in Florida, all eight of us students from the Moldovan exchange program were put on a bus on one of the very first evenings and taken to Pleasure Island, the entertainment district at Disney World. Coming from Moldova, a country where power laws forced energy conservation and the streets were pitch black at night, I was not prepared for how shocking or beautiful Pleasure Island was. Everything was bright, and everywhere you turned there were more and more lights; I thought the whole United States must be like this. I learned later that it is not.

Only a few days after my arrival to the US, on August 15, 1994, I would meet the love of my life, Jazmina, at a UCF International Student Association meeting. I found myself speaking to her for almost the entire time; our conversations flowed so easily and in a way that I had never experienced before. She was not like any of my former girlfriends, so I was not expecting what came next: that night, I saw her in my dreams.

I picked up this girl I had just met and held her in my arms. We followed a road that slid down, but as the road sloped sharply up, I heard a voice in my ear whisper, "This is your fate." I can still vividly picture waking up that next morning, clearly remembering the dream, and being thoroughly confused.

Just two days later, there was a trip organized for us by the International Student Association; we were all going to Busch Gardens, Tampa. With a two-hour drive, we had to carpool with students that had cars, and by what seemed like sheer coincidence at the time (something I now know does not exist), I rode with my other Moldovan friend and Jazmina's Turkish girlfriend in Jazmina's car. We had such fun at Busch Gardens, and within days after that trip, I came to realize that I was falling head over heels in love with this girl from Ecuador.

Jazmina and I in Bush Gardens in Tampa, Florida. This is our first picture together. It was just second time I was seeing her and it was a day after I saw the prophetic dream about her.

Jazmina and I at the Billy Joel and Elton John concert in Tampa, Florida in the Spring of 1995. Jazmina and I will see Elton John again only this time it will be from our Nutriband Corporate Suite at Amway Arena in April of 2022.

Aprilie 2022, Nutriband Inc. Presidential Suite.
Elton John farewell concert in Orlando, Florida.

During this time at UCF, I did have a girlfriend back in Moldova—the last time I ever saw her was when she said goodbye at the train station as I left for America. I knew it wasn't meant to be though, as Jazmina and I clicked at every level. We could not stop talking to each other, spending hours on the phone; everything I was learning about her was completely fascinating. Jazmina was the woman I was meant to marry, just as I was foretold in my dream and just like the wish I made as a 9 year-old boy.

In fall of 1994, while still an exchange student at UCF, Octavian Chiriac, Nicoleta Muntean, and I were interviewed by a Moldovan journalist that was to be aired in Moldova. Funny enough, Jazmina was present during the interview, hiding in a corner of our dorm room and watching us answer questions. The journalist asked one very interesting question, and I have always been surprised by my answer as a 22 year old. The question was: "Do you guys want to go back to Moldova or stay in the USA?" Both Octavian and Nicoleta adamantly asserted their intent to go home and help the country develop to become "a real European country."

"Not me," I said. "My biggest fear is that in twenty years, I will become indifferent and corrupt just like the leaders of Moldova."

My assessment was that I did not believe that the people who were running my country at the time were always like that; they were also once young, idealistic students with big dreams. Only after years of being in the system did they become who they were: victims of a very dangerous paradigm that can dramatically alter your reality and expectations.

In 2014, I saw a glimpse of what could have been my future when I helped a friend and law school colleague of mine, a judge who was running away from problems in Moldova. I hosted him and his family for about six months, and in that time, I realized he was a shell of the man I remembered from thirty years before. In school, we discussed and argued about Freudian theory, philosophy, and modern social economic problems, but he had now become somewhat shallow and uninteresting. He was visibly shaken and scared by the trouble back home, almost acting on some kind of animal instincts that were uncharacteristic of someone who sat on the bench. He told me horror stories of what he had been a part of and wanted me to understand and side with him, but I just could not. As he spoke, my skin crawled at the thought of what I could have become had I chosen to make a career in Moldova. Even now, I would like to think that apart from the battle scars of life, I have remained the same 22 year old during my interview.

In large part, America has enabled me to hold onto my values and expand my life in ways I can be proud of; I experienced this during my time in UCF's exchange program. I found studying at UCF to be much easier than my time in law school as most of the exams were multiple choice. I could read the material once and still get passing grades. As those grades were not counting towards my law degree, I did not mind what grades I actually received. The only class I truly cared about was the Spanish course I took for my spring semester in 1995. I had spent Christmas and New Year's Eve with Jazmina and her family in Ecuador, invigorating me to learn the Spanish language. I thought that my knowledge of Romanian would make it easier for me to understand Spanish as another Romance language, but this was not the case.

When we returned from Ecuador, the first thing I did was enroll in the Level III Spanish course. My first class was a disaster as all of the students had a basic understanding of Spanish and could speak to some degree; I knew nothing. The professor, Señora Katusik, picked up on this right away and approached me at the end of the first class. I told her the truth: I had never taken a Spanish class before. She recommended I start with the level I course, but I told her I couldn't: my program was finishing in May, and I only had four months to become fluent in Spanish before I went back home. Señora Katusik stared at me in disbelief until she said, "Well, if I can make a miracle, we will see..."

I took the course very seriously as I wanted to be able to speak Spanish with Jazmina; four months later, while the rest of the class was still reading by sounding out syllables and struggling to hold meaningful conversations, I was fluent and living the dream! Señora Katusik gave me an A in the class, and I believe it was the only one I received during the exchange program.

After the program ended in May 1995, I went back to Moldova to pass my final exams at the Moldova State University and start work for the bank, IntreprinzBanca. I knew I had to get back to the US, and with this goal in mind, I was able to get my former boss, Vechyaslav Vizir, to sponsor my education at UCF, studying for a master's degree in applied economics.

I had a very good relationship with Vechyaslav, who was the son of the bank's president; he really did believe in me and truly wanted to see me succeed. Unfortunately, after I left for the US, he got into a quarrel with high-ranking officials that led to a series of investigations organized by the government. This led to the bank's downfall, and both father and son were arrested and charged for corruption. The whole financial system was just being set up at the time, so some of the rules were not clear or well defined. I thought their punishment was extremely severe for the charges brought against them.

My former boss spent 11 years behind bars, and once he was released, I was able to meet with him. In my memory, he remained a 35-year-old former Air Force officer, handsome and strong, but when I met him after his release, he was a broken man. It was sad for me to see him like this, especially because his efforts helped me get into UCF for my master's degree in 1997. Without his sponsorship, it would not have been possible at that time.

When I was in my third year of law school, I had a vivid dream that the university had introduced advanced math in the law school program. I woke up in a panic, and I immediately told my roommates, the two Igors, about it; we all had a good laugh. Well, that math nightmare came true when I earned my master's degree in applied economics. During school, I was having to deal with derivatives, the Phillips curve, and statistics on a level that I hadn't experienced before, which tested my abilities. The first statistics class I took was in the class of Professor Soskin, whose lessons I struggled to understand due to his teaching style. In class, I could not understand anything he was saying, so I decided to pay more attention to the textbook; the textbook, however, was written by the same Professor Soskin. When reading it, I could hear the flow of his voice and still understood absolutely nothing.

I never had this problem in other classes as I have a phenomenal memory and practically remember entire textbooks after reading them just a few times. With Professor Soskin and statistics, I couldn't use my normal strategy of absorbing as much information as possible and then applying it later. The first out of three total exams for the semester, I failed with a D, sending me into a full panic. This was a master's degree program: I do not believe you could get a C in any of the classes, and maintaining a minimum B average was a must.

Feeling the pressure, I went to see Professor Soskin and asked for his help, honestly telling him I had a problem with his course and needed some pointers. His advice to me was unhelpful: he told me that the master's in applied economics is a very challenging program and that it might be above my intellectual level to pursue. Having graduated in the top five of my class from law school and being fluent in four languages, I had never been insulted by anyone so outright before and the last time someone insulted my intelligence was when I was in elementary school and it was Adrian Babii, my classmate. It was 1979, I was in second grade, the movie D'artanian and three Musketeers was just aired on Soviet TV and all the boys were playing the musketeers game. The coolest boy in our class was Artur Scripnic, he took the role of D'artanian, thanks to his chubby structure, Adrian Babii took the role of Partos and I requested to be Atos… Adrian's opinion was very kind and diplomatic, that it would not be the appropriate role for me as Atos was the unsung leader of the pack, he was at the center of all the planning and the intrigues… Even at the tender age of 8 I understood that Adrian was telling me in kind words that I am not fit for such a role as I am not smart enough, and what is striking to me that I still do remember such details.

I thanked professor Soskin for his time and left without knowing what to do next or how I would fare on the next two midterm exams.

Just as it's always done, the universe provided in a critical moment: I befriended a Turkish student from the same class, Husein Turhanguil. He was the son of a very important politician and chief of a faction in the Turkish parliament that just successfully impeached the prime minister of Turkey, Tansu Cillerr, a year before. This had nothing to do with statistics, but the fact that Husein graduated from the best mathematical university in Turkey had. Husein helped to tutor me; his explanations were so simple that it all started to make sense for me, and I indeed aced the next two midterms.

At the last exam, after I aced the second exam, Soskin sat by me, almost as if he thought I had to be cheating to save my grades. Well, about 15 minutes into the exam, I was the only one to find a problem in one of his multiple choice questions as it contained two correct answers and not one as implied by the problem. As he was sitting by me, it was easy for me to point out the error. After he listened to me, he went to the blackboard without saying a word and asked for the class's attention. He told them to ignore that particular problem as it had an erroneous answer. He did not come back to sit by me after that... School was a whirlwind of challenge and success. It's incredible to look back on now.

My life had changed so quickly in just a few years as I went from working at the mechanics shop and studying for law school to studying applied economics in Florida. The biggest change came when Jazmina and I married on December 21, 1996 in her home country of Ecuador (thanks to financial support from my parents).

As a wedding present, my parents gave us $3,000, an exorbitant amount of money in those days, and my father-in-law allowed us to live in his vacation home in Orlando while I studied at UCF. Nobody would use the community pool at the vacation home, so I was able to study for my classes, basking in the sun by the pool. It was more than I could have ever hoped for. As incredible life in the United States was, it wasn't all glamor and flashing lights like Pleasure Island.

While at UCF, I worked at a local McDonald's from 5 am to 3 pm for $4.75 an hour before going to school from 6 pm to 9 pm. We got discounts on food, but I couldn't afford to waste what little pay I got, so instead, I would stash breakfast burritos in my pocket and hide in the freezer to eat my meals away from the prying eyes of managers and security cameras. The money we had was spent on all the necessities to live in Florida and go to school.

To further save money, I bought an Audi 4000 from my sister's ex-boyfriend for $1,500, but I should have realized that I was being ripped off since only three doors and one window opened. At every toll booth, I had to open the door because the driver's window did not roll down. Even years later, when I went to pay at tolls in working cars, I still found myself completely opening the door to throw coins in.

When all was said and done—after the car insurance, the car title, tuition, and school supplies— Jazmina and I were down to $100 by January of 1997. As stressful as this was, I was proud of myself for how far I had come and felt so lucky to have found Jazmina. With my education and experiences, I was ready to enter a world of business in America; I just had no idea what kind of work I would be getting myself into next.

CHAPTER 3:
The Boiler Room

Since leaving Moldova, I could feel my world opening up and expanding, from exploring Florida to visiting Ecuador with Jazmina. To keep living in the United States though, I was up against the struggle of trying to find a H-1B visa, which meant holding onto a job that would be able to sponsor me until I could get a green card. I had a limited amount of time left at the University of Central Florida as a student, and the pressure was on to find work after school. Luckily, I was able to get a little help from my friends.

Octavian Chiriac was among the initial group of Moldovans that came to UCF in August of 1994, and he was also my first roommate after I roomed with my friend, Viorel Portar, during the exchange program. While I finished law school in Moldova, he stayed at UCF to get a master's degree in business administration, so by the time I graduated, he had been out in the world, working in New York City. He knew of my struggle to find a job that would sponsor my visa and did his best to help me out.

When I was finishing my degree in applied economics, Octavian was able to get me a job offer for a firm in Manhattan with a $90,000 annual salary. At the time, I was working a job for $10 an hour, and most entry-level jobs out of school had a starting salary closer to $36,000, even if you had a master's degree. Excited at the prospect of working for a hedge fund in New York City, I flew north to the city to meet with the company, only to be greeted with New York's November weather. It was constantly raining, and I was reminded of Moldova's weather, which I detested, especially after living in bright and sunny Florida.

I asked Octavian if this job was a good deal: was the money worth it? He warned me that I would have to live like him, which meant taking the train into the city every day. He couldn't afford to live in Manhattan, so he lived in Connecticut, taking the train an hour each way, on top of taking the time to park and with an overall three hour commute each day. I knew I couldn't live like this. At the time, I was spending my days finishing work by 3 or 4 pm and then relaxing by the pool, and I didn't want to exchange this lifestyle for one of stressful commutes and cold winters, no matter how good the money was.

I decided to take my chances by finding my next job on my own, but this was harder than I thought it would be. I went from interview to interview, ready to take the plunge into a new position, but as soon as I brought up that I needed a sponsor for my H-1B visa, the tone of the interviews shifted. I would see the members of the meetings' faces change, and they would immediately say I was "overqualified" for the position. I started to become more desperate as companies were unwilling to sponsor my visa, and Jazmina needed to find a work visa as well, being from Ecuador. I had only a year after the optional training once I had graduated from university, and then my employment authorization would expire.

Finally, Octavian came to me again, and this time, he knew of an opportunity with a company he had experience with in Florida. The proximity was crucial, but more importantly, they were willing to sponsor my visa. In 1999, I went to the interview in Altamonte Springs. I had no idea what this company did or what was going on, but I sat down with a man and woman, both from Puerto Rico, who were incredibly nice. They hired me as an analyst, and to be quite honest, I still had no real idea what the company did as I left the interview; I just knew that my visa was sponsored and I had a job.

Looking back, I wish I had known what a boiler room was, but the overall experience was incredibly formative to my business sensibilities.

With the Internet boom, there were so many companies that were hitting the market at $10 to $15 a stock, but the stocks we were working with did not have the financial statements to back up their value. My job was to analyze these companies for brokers who sold stocks on the phone. On paper, there was incredible technology being developed, but it turns out it was all fraudulent: everything was a lie.

There was one medical company that claimed to have plenty of new technology and five trucks to ship their products around the country, all while generating great revenue. When I spoke to one of the brokers though, he told me that this company had nothing—they didn't even have one truck, let alone five. Another company was said to have developed a new material that was impenetrable to fire and radiation. These stocks were trading at $2 and $3, never going higher, because as another broker told me, "If a stock is a $2 price, then it deserves to be a $2 price." I find it funny that, to this day, I still remember the companies and their symbols: BLTD, FFCI, LIFR, KRHL...

Companies were not subject to periodic filings, so you could trade on the OTC Bulletin Board and have a quote on active market makers; plus, company financials did not have to be audited. You could say anything you wanted, so it was very tough to understand what was real and what was not. I started out analyzing these companies and determining what was real, but soon, I had the responsibilities of cold calling and teaching other brokers. Every stock, I found out, was a lie; without fail, every stock went from $10 to a penny within six months, and so many people lost money.

One of the brokers, Barry, invested $50,000 into what would become a failing stock, buying in at $9 a share and higher on my recommendation. I warned him to sell at $3 a share, but he decided to keep it until the very end. Eventually, he lost every penny he invested with me. He had to sell his home and move into an apartment, and his life crumbled around him. I felt horrible and guilty, and I tried to do everything I could to help him, but in the end, it didn't matter. He wasn't the only one this happened to; there were so many others.

One after another, our projects began to fold, and I finally understood the game of the boiler room. I found it harder and harder to pitch the stories behind these fake companies as we read off of false market analysis, so my sales inevitably began to drop. I was barely making the cut at the end of each month, but I had to stay in the job so they would sponsor my visa. Misleading people ate at my insides, but in turn, it sparked a revelation for me: if I could get investors interested in these fake companies, why couldn't I do the same with real companies?

I saw the potential to take real fledgling companies public and be transparent with them about the whole process. At this point, I was still young and inexperienced, so I had no real clue what that whole process was, but I knew I didn't want to be like these crooks I was working with, who just took the money and ran.

A friend of mine, another broker, offered up a position at First Union Securities. They were willing to sponsor my work visa, except I would have to pass the tests for a Series 7 license. Luckily, I was fired from the boiler room and immediately began studying for my Series 7 tests to become a financial broker. This felt like a real opportunity to turn things around after the boiler room, so I dedicated myself to hustling and passing the tests. To be able to feed myself, I got a job at Papa John's delivering pizzas from 5 pm to late in the evening, four days a week, and making about as much money as I had as an analyst.

Every morning, I studied old Xerox copies of a Series 7 book because I couldn't get my hands on an expensive study book. Finally, it paid off: I was able to pass the exams with an 80% and start working with First Union Securities.

At First Union Securities, I was surrounded by very high-profile brokers who had large clients that were investing vast amounts of money. I'd watch them buy everything and then quickly turn around and sell it without following any real science behind it. I soon realized they were not that different from the boiler room; even if the market turned really bad and everybody was losing money, you still had to make those cold calls and put clients into stocks you were not confident about anymore.

Again, I felt trapped and didn't like the job, but it was what I had in the moment, working around all of these other people who were two-faced in their business dealings. Little did I know, I had been working closely with a con man in my own personal deals.

CHAPTER 4:
Vadim and Asconi

———•———

When I first met Vadim Enikeev, before working at the boiler room, I was introduced by a friend at a meeting of Russian expatriates, and to say that I was impressed by him is an understatement. Vadim was a multimillionaire with a PhD from Columbia University, driving the latest Jaguar at the time and wearing a $30,000 Rolex Presidential, while I was barely out of school, struggling to find work and keep my visa. It was a brief encounter, but the image of him in my mind was cemented; he was around my age, yet he had achieved so much in such a short amount of time.

I did not see Vadim again until I was working as a financial advisor at First Union Securities, where he opened up an account with me, putting in $10,000. While I was managing his money, I enjoyed his company as he was an exciting figure to be around, constantly talking about multimillion-dollar deals or the countless connections he had with successful business people. We slowly became friends, but it almost felt inevitable because he had such an aura around him that you couldn't help but be pulled into his charm.

As we grew closer, he started bringing clients into First Union Securities to open up accounts, and we became more comfortable working together. Eventually, I opened up to him about my new dream of bringing companies public, and he was incredibly supportive, wanting to partner with me on these deals.

Eventually, it took some time, but I got it: People that are honest do not talk of their honesty. People who are loyal do not brag about how loyal they can be. People who are rich do not talk about how much money they have. Scoundrels do. Working with Vadim, the signs were present the entire time, but I was too young and fresh to see them for what they were—the dealings of a scammer. The first time I was suspicious was when he brought in a client from Russia, a big-time figure from the Administration of the President of the Russian Federation. She personally knew Vladimir Putin and had arrived in Orlando to meet with me about opening an investment with First Union Securities. Before she arrived at the office, I received a call from Vadim that was simultaneously confusing and unbelievable. He informed me that he had told this woman from Russia that he was the owner of First Union Securities. Understandably confused, I immediately asked him to repeat what he had said over the phone, and he repeated his lie, eventually hanging up.

Looking back, the proper thing to do would have been to call off the meeting, but I had no idea what I was going to do at that moment. There was no *one* owner of First Union Securities as it was a multibillion-dollar company with countless shareholders, and Vadim had no official role with the company either way. I couldn't contradict Vadim; otherwise, I would be throwing him under the bus and jeopardizing the deal. When the Russian woman asked me if Vadim was actually the owner of the company, I immediately downplayed his role, saying he was a "part-owner of the office," and I left it at that. This move of his, forcing me to go along with his last-minute lies meant to impress, became familiar as I continued to work with him.

Some of my first clients as a Series 7 broker were the partners, Anatol Sirbu and Constantin Jitaru, from the Asconi Winery in Moldova, who were recommended to me by my brother-in-law at the time. Vadim and I were interested in taking Asconi public and began courting them. I was still incredibly inexperienced at the time and had no clue how to take a company public, so I instinctively let Vadim handle most of the negotiations. He is, to this day, the best salesperson I have ever met; he had everyone wrapped around his finger. He would speak with such confidence and conviction to these businessmen who were older than both of us, talking to them as if he was already in control of Asconi.

Vadim just had a charm and charisma that you could not teach; he made you feel like a close friend, but there was always an air of mystery about him.

At one point, we needed to get a visa for an American to get into Russia for a business trip. I watched as Vadim entered the Russian embassy with the American, flashing his identification of "the advisor to the President of the Russian Federation," and within a half an hour, they came out with a visa. If he wanted something, Vadim could make it happen, and I saw this firsthand.

Consulting with us on the initial public offering were a collection of investment bankers, one of which was a man named Thomas Tedrow, who I would later work for. Vadim told me to take a backseat during the negotiations because I, still being a Series 7 broker at the time, created a conflict of interest. We would then split everything in half like we had discussed, but I was still not comfortable with this agreement. I was not sure if he possessed the knowledge to pull off this deal, especially when he still found it necessary to lie during our Asconi negotiations, saying he was the owner of the Delano Hotel in Miami. Still, against my better judgment, I agreed to let him take control of the situation.

While I was preparing to go on a road trip through Moldova with one of the potential investment bankers, I received a worrying call from Vadim. The lawyers were already moving ahead with a straightforward registration offering on Asconi, but Vadim told me he was flying to Texas because Thomas Tedrow, our client, had found a good trading shell for the deal.

This was a red flag to me, and I told him this struck me as a huge mistake. I asked him, "What do you know about shells?" He didn't know how many shares would be available or what was in the shell, how much debt it had, what liabilities it carried, etc. There was no due diligence done whatsoever, and he was just going to sign the deal anyway. He started yelling that he was the one in charge, and he was going to do it, whether they wanted it or not. I turned to my brother-in-law, who had referred Asconi to me as a client, and warned him of what was going on, but he told me not to make much noise around it, saying, "Let's see what happens."

I wanted to warn Anatol and Constantin asconi's owners, but they had already signed over the power of attorney to Vadim, so there was nothing I could do. Vadim was clever to ask me to present him as the "go-to guy," and at that critical moment, I was of no importance—my opinion did not matter. He had been the face of the entire operation, working closely with everyone, even though they were technically my clients from the start. Still, I was trapped in a mess of my own making, praying to be liberated, but that liberation would not come soon enough.

I arranged countless meetings with Vadim and I as corporate promoters, including with the president of Moldova, President Voronin at the time. I still have a picture in my home office of Enikeev, Tedrow, and I with the president, spreading the word about Asconi. Meeting the president of Moldova was part of a due diligence trip we embarked on after Vadim signed the Asconi Corporation into the shell company that Tedrow had pitched to him.

Ringing the opening bell for the American Stock Exchange on behalf of Asconi on November 4, 2003. Asconi was the first Moldovan Company successfully listed on a Major Stock Exchange and I was the first Moldovan that was presented the honour to ring the opening bell.

All the while, the stock continued an upward trend, trading around $7 and $9, yet there were volumes of shares flooding the market less than a month after the reverse merger. Vadim and I had received our portion of shares, but there was a large amount of restricted stock that could not be traded for at least a year after it was issued. It wasn't until I went to the First Union Securities offices and looked up all the filings on the Asconi deal that I realized what had happened.

Vadim had signed everything the bankers had wanted him to without fully understanding what he had signed. I believe the shell company involved in the reverse merger was called Grand Slam Treasures, and it was engaged in finding treasure throughout the world's oceans. If it sounds like a scam, that's because it was exactly that.

According to the deal, our Asconi clients were supposed to maintain a majority of the company, around 80%, but when I ran the numbers, Asconi was only left with about 30%. Vadim had issued 1.6 million S-8 shares amongst the four parties of bankers and consultants, while the Asconi clients, Vadim, and myself received none. These S-8 shares could be traded as soon as the bankers wanted, so they immediately started flooding the market with these shares, making millions of dollars within months of closing the deal. Anatol and Constantin, who had spent their lives building up the winery, had been screwed out of their company, and I was partially to blame.

The sense of betrayal I felt was overwhelming as I could not trust anyone at this point beyond my clients at Asconi. The investment bankers were misleading us from the start, while Vadim had been lying to me at every turn. I called Anatol and Constantin to explain what had happened, telling them to come to the United States immediately. I offered to get a lawyer for them, feeling a sense of responsibility to make things right, and I even paid their $15,000 retainer. Constantin was the only one that came to the US during this time, and I was there to assist in untangling the Gordian Knot that I inadvertently created. After we met the lawyers and had a clear map of moving forward, Asconi told me that I should work for them, but I would have to give back all of my initial shares. To make matters worse, I still did not have a green card and needed to be sponsored by the company for my H-1B visa.

This felt like too much leverage over me since they could fire me at any moment and take everything away with a snap of their fingers, and I found it to be a bad deal. About a week later, after Constantin returned to Moldova, I received the lawsuit from the Asconi owners, lumping me in with Vadim and the investment bankers. It was one of the most stressful experiences I've ever had in business. I punched the wall in the kitchen of my father-in-law's vacation home so hard that my fist went completely through to the other side, knocking the kitchen phone off the wall. I was being sued for so much money, and I had brought everything on myself.

I was the one who introduced Vadim to Asconi and kickstarted this whole process, so everything he and the bankers were accused of—conspiracy to commit fraud, conspiracy to defraud them of assets, breach of fiduciary duties—they accused of me as well. I had no assets or resources to handle this lawsuit, and it wasn't until I had help from one of the accused investment bankers, Thomas Tedrow, that I had a fighting chance (though his help came at a price).

Vadim had been exposed for all of his lies, including not actually having a PhD from Columbia University, among other things, so he also had to deal with the lawsuit with limited resources. Instead of facing the lawsuit, he fled by joining the US Army. Only a few months later, September 11 shook the world, and he was shipped to Iraq.

Vadim was the only one who did not even try to defend himself, so soon after the lawsuit was initiated, Vadim got a default judgment against him for the whole amount of $12 million. I eventually ended up helping him settle with Asconi and strike down the judgment against him. He was still in the army at the time, so I was dealing with his ex-wife during this process.

After that, I wouldn't talk to Vadim until 2007, when I had an incredibly vivid dream about him and he called me just a few days later. We caught up and rekindled our friendship for a period, even going as far as starting a soccer team together in Central Florida, winning multiple cups and championships.

He offered to work with me again and again, but I adamantly refused; instead, I recommended lawyers and accountants to help him with his latest project. Vadim being Vadim, he could not stay out of trouble for long. His project was a Russian company he took public, and when it began to trade, he gave into temptation. You need to wait at least one year before you are able to make any money off of the stocks, but not for Vadim.

We had offices next to each other at a corporate hub before he moved. At the time, I didn't know where, but a mailing mistake sent an invoice meant for him to my office. It was the first payment of an Aston Martin for over $4,000. I was able to track Vadim down through my contacts and went to see him personally. What can I say? I was intrigued.

My suspicions were fully justified after I saw his new office. Only he and the bank occupied the magnificent, huge, first floor of the First Union Building. I saw plenty of young students working there, only to find out that Vadim was hiring them for three-month, non-pay trial periods. After they served their time, he would fire them and hire others. I learned the rent for the office was astronomical, and his Russian investors were paying for his office expenses. I realized that Vadim was selling his stock for personal gains to maintain a price and volume in the market, and I immediately called all of my contacts that I had introduced to him. I warned them his project had only three to six months before it would crash hard, and sure enough, after two months, it crashed to pennies. After the summer of 2009, Vadim disappeared, and I didn't hear any news about him until 2014.

Eventually, Vadim's crimes caught up to him in Russia. I learned he had been arrested for printing counterfeit certificates and selling them as shares in a US company that planned an IPO in the US financial markets, thereby defrauding more than $50 million from Russian investors. He and his accomplices were living large on the investors' money, buying exotic cars and motorcycles and even displaying some of them in their offices. The Russian FSB captured all of his conspirators in 2014, and he was sentenced to nine years in jail.

If I met Vadim again, I would still talk to him and probably even enjoy our conversation, even after his time in Russian prison. I owe a lot of my own success to working with him because he threw me into the deep end; I gained confidence in my own power and abilities because I was pushed to a limit I had never expected to reach. If it weren't for him, I would probably still be a lowly financial advisor with a decent paying job, not doing anything noteworthy or exciting. Working with Vadim was just the tip of the iceberg though as it kickstarted one of the most extraordinary chess games of my life against Thomas Tedrow.

CHAPTER 5:
Thomas and the Asconi Lawsuit

It was very hard to hate Thomas Tedrow. Even though I knew he'd been involved in some shady deals and was partially to blame for the Asconi lawsuit, he had an undeniable charm about him—he was always incredibly nice and polite, and I do remember him fondly.

Thomas had an undeniable charm about him—he was the kind of guy who was in a rock band when he was younger; presenting himself as cool and likable came easily. Besides being an investment banker, he had also written a series of children books and their screenplay adaptations. He had a beautiful wife, beautiful children, and an incredible home. It was the dream goal. At the time I met him, he was about the same age I am now. If I would have had any role model at the time, it would be Thomas, no doubt.

When he talked to you, you felt seen and heard, so I can only blame myself for being misled with the Asconi deal. You only go as far as someone leads you. Even in his handshake, Thomas was particular; he would always use his left hand to cover the right hand of the person he shakes hands with to make them feel extra appreciated. It worked.

Unfortunately, I was led straight into a $12 million lawsuit with Asconi, which believed I betrayed the company's leadership during what should have been their crowning achievement.

Before the lawsuit, while the deal was still good, Thomas had offered me a job to work at his firm and I was reluctant to accept it as I was looking to get a position at Asconi. I had quit First Union Securities weeks before, and I was not looking forward to going back there. When we were all struck by the lawsuit, I was in a dire position: I had no job, I had a pending visa that was about to run out, and I had no money. I went to Thomas to see if I could still work for him, and he accepted me, either because he liked my work or he wanted to keep me close during the lawsuit.

I worked as a consultant for Thomas, bringing in new deals to his firm, but this was extremely stressful as I was relying on him for my work visa. I was reluctant with every deal I brought in, and I couldn't shake a feeling of anxiety, knowing full well how Thomas took advantage of Asconi. He was among the four investment bankers that issued themselves 1.6 million shares in Asconi before flooding the market with them. I knew it would only be a matter of time before Thomas would try to use me for the lawsuit in some way.

I didn't have my own lawyer when Asconi sued us, but Thomas was able to provide me with one, even paying the retainer for me as I had no money. The lawyer wrote the request for dismissal, but after that, I soon realized that she was not a very good lawyer or at least not very invested in my case. My financial situation only grew more grim as I now had to pay for a new lawyer, but I had no resources to fight back.

In this incredibly low period for me, I did the only thing I could do: I approached Thomas Tedrow to sell my shares in Asconi. I was desperate, and he knew this, but I was willing to sell them for whatever price he would pay, even though the stock was trading around $4. With the lock-up period still in place after the IPO, Thomas offered me $40,000 for 100,000 shares, and with no other option, I sold him one of my certificates for ten times less than the market price at the time.

With Thomas' firm, I worked on a couple of big clients for him, all from Moldova, including another wine company, an agricultural company, and an oil company. I did my due diligence, gathering and organizing all of the materials for the audits of these companies, but I was incredibly worried that I might have another Asconi on my hands. If these deals fell apart from Thomas Tedrow's touch, there was no way I could return to Moldova, having burned two companies at the hands of the same man.

During all of this, I still made time to be an athlete and play soccer, get my second dan black belt in Taekwondo, and refresh my Judo skills, but I began uncontrollably gaining weight in a way that was unusual. My skin also started to break out, and I was unsure of what could have been causing all of these sudden health problems. I soon found out that the stress of the lawsuit, losing money I never had, and working for Thomas was so intense it destroyed my thyroid gland. To this day, I still need to take pills for my thyroid, but the damage was done.

I learned a lot from Vadim about confidence as I was thrown into the deep end and forced to swim in the aftermath of the Asconi deal, but with Thomas, I learned the finesse of business, like perfecting my backstroke. I noticed he had an absolute separation between his personal life and business. I think I took this to heart; I did my best to keep much of the Asconi deal and the lawsuit from Jazmina as I didn't want to mess up the only place I was free from stress: home. I knew I had to find a way out of this mess, but I was unsure of what options I really had.

Working at Thomas' firm was a young man around my age named Jacob, who was very close to Thomas but incredibly kind to me. I was surprised Jacob wanted to work on all of my deals and be in business with me without me asking, which worked in my favor. He gave me important insight into my certificate sale to Thomas, which was a moment of desperation for me but a great deal for Thomas. Jacob told me that while I sold Thomas my shares for ten cents per share, Thomas was able to turn around and sell my shares for about fifty cents a share.

I had been expecting that kind of behavior from Thomas, but even still, this incensed me to no end. Thomas was nice enough in his day to day, but that separation of personal issues and work allowed him to have a ferocious business approach: if he could take 100% of the deal, he would take 100% of the deal. He would not be shy about it, and I knew that if I was going to get out of this situation, it would take a lot of cunning on my part to match him. I was playing the most difficult chess games of my life, and the only way I could win was by cheating.

Luckily, I had made an important ally at the firm — Thomas trusted Jacob so implicitly that Jacob had access to all of Thomas' computer passwords and emails. Jacob shared a lot of information with me, especially with emails concerning the lawsuit and what Thomas' next moves would be. I was playing with fire, but with my back against the wall, I knew I had no other choice if I was to free myself from Thomas' hold over me. Thomas had kept me close this entire time, but I knew he would throw me to the curb if it meant he could get out of the lawsuit unscathed. As unbelievably lucky as I was to have access to his emails, it didn't sit well with me then, and it doesn't sit well with me now. I still carry that guilt, but I don't regret that I was able to protect myself and my family.

I consider working behind Thomas Tedrow's back with Jacob's access to his emails as an extreme low, but it was absolutely necessary at the time. I was recovering from Vadim's betrayal while under Thomas' thumb, and with no allies backing me up in this fight, what choice did I have?

It was the fall of 2002, and time was of the essence as I suddenly felt that my days at Tedrow's office were numbered. First, I needed Asconi to settle me out completely. I approached the lawyer who Thomas had initially hired for me and told her that there was a big conflict of interest between me and Asconi's lawyers. Not only had I introduced them and spilled all of the details on the case, but I also paid their $15,000 retainer. With almost $400,000 sunk in lawyer fees, there was no way Asconi could just switch to another lawyer. If they were able to get a new lawyer, they would have to spend at least $25,000 to catch that lawyer up to speed. I knew I had gotten their attention.

The lawsuit had been dragging on with no real end in sight, but my brother-in-law had been making moves of his own. He was speaking with the team at Asconi over Christmas of 2002 and was able to arrange a meeting with Constantin and Anatol for me. I flew to Moldova in January of 2003 and laid out my entire plan that had been brewing up to that moment.

I made a promise to Asconi: I would end the lawsuit to stop legal expenses and settle everybody out, but they would have to let me restructure their company and bring them to the major market. I asked for a carte blanche in my actions, and I got one. I think at this point in the lawsuit, the deal looked like a light at the end of the tunnel to them, so they took a leap of faith and trusted me.

The next step was to settle everybody else out, but I was strategic with my tactics since I had access to Thomas' emails with the lawyers. I had let them spend enough money on the lawyers for the past year, but I knew that with everything stalled, they wouldn't want to draw this out any longer than they had to.

One by one, I settled out everyone from the lawsuit with them paying about $100,000 each to settle and Vadim giving back all of his shares but 10,000 (that became 1,000 after the reverse split 1:10), but I saved Thomas Tedrow for last. When I approached Thomas, I told him that everybody else had settled, and now it was us against him. In the end, Thomas paid about $250,000 in combined stock and cash, the most out of anyone involved in the lawsuit.

With my two years working under Thomas, I was finally free, and I now had the opportunity to restructure Asconi and bring them to market; my entire world had just opened up. I also understood that I could never work with Jacob, even though his help at the time made it possible for me to break free from Thomas. Someone who would betray so easily a person that unconditionally trusted him for years and assured him a nice level of living with a high six figure salary, would not think twice about betraying someone like me.

Somehow, the lawsuit did not interrupt my green card application, which Thomas could have easily messed up, but the paperwork was already in motion. Not having to constantly fight to keep a visa would later make my life so much easier.

Thomas and I were able to bury the hatchet a couple of months later. We centered Asconi's offices in Winter Park, Florida, not far from Thomas' offices, so he came to visit and talk. We realized that the chess game we had been playing, stalking around each other, was over. I did end up doing another deal with him, but I made sure that I was the escrow, holding onto the money and paying everything according to the terms. He was not to be trusted, and if you asked me to do a deal with him now, I probably would not. Tom is one of the most formidable opponents I ever had to play against.

Ahead of me was a great opportunity to bring Asconi to market, just like I had promised them and myself. I told a dream I had to Constantin at the height of the lawsuit; it was a vivid dream of being stuck in a dark cellar, shuffling around looking for a key to open the door and escape. At the end of the dream, I reached into my pocket, realizing I had the key the entire time. Just like how Vadim's influence on me gave me the courage to take deals head on, my navigation around Thomas Tedrow was a reminder that I had the power in me to take on adversity.

I was ready to make my biggest deal yet, but I had no idea what battles were ahead of me.

CHAPTER 6:
Uplisting Asconi on the American Stock Exchange

———————•———————

Overcoming the lawsuit from Asconi took an incredible amount of energy, but having earned the company's trust back, I was prepared to follow through on my promise of restructuring them. Asconi had spent a lot of money on the lawyers, and though the stock had dropped to a penny stock since they started the lawsuit, I, as director of the company, was determined to bring them to the American Stock Exchange.

When I offered Constantin and Anatol my plan in January 2003, I think they were skeptical of how I was going to actually revive Asconi. I started with a reverse stock split and divided the outstanding shares, including Asconi's family shares in the market, by ten, so we could ultimately lift the stock price from $0.40 to $4 per share. My family was in the possession of 300,000 shares, and another 100,000 shares were issued to me as Asconi's employee, while Constantin and Anatol were issued five million shares each.

After consolidating the shares, the real work began: public relations, investor relations, finalizing the lawsuit, and the application to AMEX. It was work that I took pride in, knowing that I was spearheading the efforts to effectively save this Moldovan wine company. While applying to the American Stock Exchange, we received an opinion from

Asconi's lawyer, Jeffery Bahnsen—the same lawyer who I brought to Asconi in 2001 and who was instrumental in filing the lawsuit against myself and others involved in the deal—that the shares issued to Constantin and Anatol were to be treated as founders shares, which, in a nutshell, meant no financial hit on the balance sheet.

The stock was $4 at the time of the issuance, so it would have meant a $40 million charge on the income statement. The analyst from AMEX accepted the opinion when our independent auditors at the time, Michelson and Co., did. Three months after we began the filing process, we qualified on all AMEX standards, including the fundamentals, the stock price, and the shareholders. We needed to close at $4.75 the day before to qualify, and we did exactly that. On November 4, 2003, I rang the opening bell at the American Stock Exchange and was able to introduce the Moldovan wine company to the largest market in the world.

Meeting Vladimir Voronin, the third President of the Republic of Moldova (center second from right) with Vadim Enikeev (first from left), Thomas Tedrow (centre left) and myself (first on the right).

We were able to accomplish this all without raising any funds, which was quite surprising. After we qualified, we raised about $2 million in a private placement, and we watched the stock price go through the roof. I was on top of the world watching the stock trading at $11 in huge volumes everyday; everything I had promised Asconi was coming true, and I made everyone at the company very happy. This feeling did not last though.

Four months after we listed, while the stock was trading high, we got an inquiry from the Securities and Exchange Commission about the treatment of the shares. I brought everyone in the company together and made it very clear that the auditing process was very serious and will come at a cost. We went step by step through the process with highly qualified consultants, one of whom worked for SEC enforcement in the past. It did not take long for us to reach the conclusion that Jeffrey Bahnsen from Greenberg and Traurig had no business issuing an opinion on the founders' shares, and the accountants and auditors had no right to rely on his opinion.

There we were with an $8 stock on AMEX, suddenly needing to restate the financials for the whole year and address the issuance of the 10 million shares to the two company principals. Even though I knew we had done honest work, I couldn't help but feel nervous. I'd worked so hard to make Asconi respectable, and yet, one challenge after another came knocking at the door.

Finally, after $200,000 in consulting fees and three months of being frozen on AMEX (because we filed 8-K of non-reliance on the financial statements in spring of 2004), we filed our restated financial statements during the summer.

We were immediately hit by class-action lawsuits, but all of the cases got voluntarily dismissed after the restatements became official.

After we filed our restated financials, we got a call from the American Stock Exchange and braced for the worst. It turned out that our consultants did such a good job with the restating that it was in line with that of a successful blue chip company. They reopened trading on the stock right away, and we were back on AMEX under the ACD symbol shortly after the company got an offer from the SEC to settle for a $50,000 slap-on-the-wrist fine. None of the directors were found at fault, but the independent auditors and the company's chief accountant at the time had received the Wells Notices from the SEC. To me, this was a big win, but to Constantin Jitaru and Anatol Sirbu, it was business as usual—nothing special.

With the class-action suits and being taken off of the exchange for three months, the stock was trading around $3, and we didn't have the same volumes as before. I knew we would have to get more interest in the stock again, and that meant hiring a PR firm and reaching out to brokers. I talked to Constantin, the CEO, about how he and Anatol were in Moldova; they did not speak English, and I was representing them and the company in all of these meetings. They had given me the title Chief Operations Officer and Director, but I told them it was more appropriate for someone in the position of president or CFO to be the representative or to get more people on the board as we were now a serious company trading on AMEX. Constantin told me, "If you want to be a president, I have a suggestion for you, Seriojica. How about you make your own company, and you become a president."

He would call me Seriojica either lovingly or sarcastically, depending on the context of the conversation. The words stung, but I took them to heart.

At this point in my relationship with Asconi, I was beginning to feel certain frustrations, especially after putting out so many of their fires. When we initially applied to AMEX, there was an annual fee of $15,000 that I paid out of pocket, and Asconi promised to pay me back. They never did end up paying me back, and to them, I was to blame for the SEC's investigation. On top of this, I had not been paid a salary for my first year of work, and though I was not struggling for money, it was the principle for me.

This mismanagement of Asconi was evident even in how the offices were run. One day, the phone lines just stopped working, and I could not figure out why this was the case. After going to the Moldovan chief accounting officer, he told me that he just wasn't paying the phone bills, which I had been covering the year before. I told him, "I've lived in this country for many years; I never *not* pay my bills."

He replied, "Well, you just never tried not to pay."

It was obvious that they were working under the Russian/ Moldovan mindset of the more you owe, the more valuable you are.

During this time with Asconi, I had other dreams for my life, including starting my own family with Jazmina. It was an incredible struggle to have kids for us, and we did all that we could to make it possible. When Jazmina first became pregnant, I was ecstatic, but my first instinct was to keep this between just Jazmina and myself. Eventually, I could not take it anymore, and I had to tell my family and friends about the good news.

At around the fifth week of the pregnancy, I had a dream that was incredibly vivid: there was a procession of men in black suits outside of my grandmother's home in Moldova. I was led down this corridor of people into the house where I found a baby laying on the table. I woke up, startled, gasping the name "Daniel" and surprising myself with this exclamation. Jazmina and I did not know if the baby was a boy or a girl, but I knew our child's name was Daniel. Not long after, Jazmina had a miscarriage, and we lost Daniel, leaving us both devastated and unsure of what our future family would look like. I did what I could to support Jazmina, but work was a nice distraction.

The SEC investigation had ended, and hiring a PR firm to rejuvenate the stock and earn the investors' confidence again was my top priority. The first three months of payments to the PR firm were necessary for us to proceed, but Asconi told me that I would have to pay the firm out of my own pocket. I was told that if they liked the work and the stock crossed the $5 threshold, then they would pay me back; otherwise, it would be my loss.

With the stock trading at about $3.75, I felt I had no choice, but I believed that the stock would get back over $5 easily, considering it had been at the $8 to $10 range before the stock freeze. With sales increasing and a hot market, I hit the road for investor presentations, and people were quick to jump on the opportunity to buy on. The stock got to the $5 level quickly, but then I noticed something strange was happening.

There was a large amount of stock selling around the $5 level; it was flooding the market, and I knew that nobody would profit by selling at that level unless they got free, or practically free, stock and then pocketed the quick cash. I knew the only ones who could really benefit would be me or the founders, so I called them, asking them to uphold their end of the bargain they'd made before. I wanted Asconi to pay me all that I was owed for my PR work, but their brief answer was that the stock did not go over $5 *consistently* as it would fall back down to around $4.75 after passing $5 every day. The call left me full of doubt, but I wanted to believe in human decency and that I had some control over the situation.

I knew that Constantin and Anatol could not be selling the shares or they would generate a filing with the SEC, which left the only other person I knew could be doing this: my ex-brother-in-law. I knew he had an offshore account under the name Brysdel Company because he had used my home address as the mailing address for that account, and I had even received paper sales orders for the stocks. I suspected he was a "front" for Constantin and Anatol, and I kept the sales orders in case I had to talk to the SEC. I estimated they sold about $500,000 worth of stock through the offshore company. To this day, I still kept all the confirmations.

I wanted to confront Constantin and Anatol, call our lawyers, and bring them to the SEC, but I was powerless. My brother-in-law would cover for them, especially that at that time my sister informed him that she wanted a divorce. Besides, Asconi partners were powerful and borderline aggressive people. Frustrated with no idea what to do next, I had to take some time away.

In the spring of 2005, I took Jazmina to Jamaica for a week, but in all honesty, it felt like three months. I cleared my mind and felt such a peace in my soul, reminiscent of my days at my grandparent's farm, and finally made my decision.

As soon as I came back to the office, I turned in my resignation. The day Asconi announced to the markets that Chief Operation Officer and Director Serguei Melnik quit, the stock fell about 50%, and within six months after my resignation, Asconi Inc.. was delisted from the American Stock Exchange. They had failed to pay AMEX their $15,000 yearly fee.

October 2005, from my Galapagos adventure. It was the moment of reflection after I quit Asconi Corporation. I was a novice in diving, freshly getting my scuba license in the fresh waters of Central Florida. My first saltwater dive was at Wolf Island in the Galapagos Archipelago, and it was tough for a newbie, with cold water, strong currents, but not as strong as I experienced at the next dive site where we were stationed for 3 days, Darwin Island. After two weeks I left Galapagos with an Advanced PADI DIVER Licence.

At a certain point, I knew I would have to move on from Asconi, so I had started my own consulting business, Wolf Blitz Inc., around 2004. My time with Asconi had not damaged my reputation, but if the company's inner workings were public knowledge, that could have been a different story. Instead, I had the opportunity to work with a range of companies, bringing them public: an Ecuadorian construction company, a Russian construction company, a Moldovan agricultural conglomerate, and even a Moldovan media company.

In 2016, the chief position of the Central Bank of Moldova opened up, and I applied, knowing that I likely wouldn't get it, but I saw the opportunity for exposure. More than 11 years after I rang the opening bell, nobody but a handful of people in Moldova knew that a Moldovan Company had been listed on Wall Street. I knew who was going to win, but I threw my hat in the ring anyway.

My plan for exposure worked though as I was all over the news and events, but I knew something was missing. I must have taken Constantin's words about "starting my own business" to heart, and despite having some very successful deals with my consulting company, I wanted more.

Luckily, I would soon make a friend and build a company that I truly believe in.

CHAPTER 7:
Gareth and Nutriband

———•———

My consulting company, Wolf Blitz Inc., became my focus after Asconi. After all of the betrayal I had experienced over the years, I wanted to be able to choose who I worked with carefully. With the companies that I brought public, I was not prepared to take on any board positions, mostly because I did not fully trust my client companies and their representatives. Otherwise, I was focused on building my family. It was an extremely fraught time as this was not an easy process for Jazmina and me.

We turned to in vitro fertilization, still saddened from losing our first baby but hopeful for the possibility of finally starting a family. After one of the eggs failed, we were left with three eggs, but suddenly, Jazmina became pregnant with twins, two boys. The boys were supposed to be born in 2008, and I was the happiest I had ever been, excited at the prospect of becoming a father to twin boys. After about five months of pregnancy, it was March 8, International Women's Day, and we were just about to go out to dinner when Jazmina's water broke; I had never expected something that drastic and horrifying to happen to us.

At the hospital, the doctors and nurses avoided giving us any information for hours until finally it was confirmed that Jazmina would give birth, but the babies would not survive. One of my biggest fears was that the babies would die unbaptized, so after consulting with a priest, I learned I could baptize them as their father. Jazmina and I lost both of our sons, and we were filled with the most excruciating pain we had ever felt. I was overwhelmed and wanted to die as all sense to my life was lost, but Jazmina and I found strength, holding each other in our arms.

Eventually, we would build up the strength to try and have children again, and we are now blessed with a son and a daughter. This journey into parenthood was arduous, but I have been able to watch my children grow in ways I could have never imagined. I've seen my son play sports with incredible skill, and my daughter has one of the most beautiful minds; it's been a treasure watching them grow.

"Jazmina" My Mother-in-law painted this picture in 2009. Jazmina and I lost our twins in March of 2008. Jazmina's Mom never explained to us the details of the painting, she said she felt like it was a good set to paint Jazmina at that time. When I look closer, I can see the silhouettes of our twins walking away from her.

With that said, I did not expect to be pulled back into the business world in such a significant way.

An opportunity arose from an unexpected place; I had a wonderful friendship with the partners at the PR company we had hired for Asconi. One of them, Dina Lyaskovitz, ended up inviting me to Las Vegas for Thanksgiving in 2015.

Thanksgiving is the one holiday in the United States that I do not understand; I love Christmas and bringing the family together, but Thanksgiving will continue to confuse me. We were to go to Jazmina's sisters that year, but I had to put my foot down and declare I wasn't going. In fact, I had planned to go scuba diving in Cancun until Dina invited me to Las Vegas to talk to a very interesting young gentleman who had an already established company and needed help growing it.

I decided to go to Vegas, knowing that I didn't want to get too wrapped up in this young man's business and would keep my relationship purely to that of a consultant. When I arrived in Las Vegas, I went to the Luxor Hotel to meet with Dina and prepare for my meeting with Gareth Sheridan the next morning.

When I first saw Gareth, it was in line at the Luxor's breakfast buffet, and his height was the first thing that struck me—as a six foot nine young man, he towered above everyone else.

He was quite shy at first, but he was able to lay out his company, Nutriband, to me with great specificity. Nutriband produces transdermal drug delivery systems in the form of patches to deliver dosages at a controlled rate, similar to nicotine patches but with many more applications. Gareth successfully developed the idea for Nutriband while completing his thesis at Dublin Institute of Technology, and it had been successful in the following years by selling vitamin supplement patches in Ireland.

Gareth was so successful, in fact, that he sold Nutriband to a company in the US for a decent amount of shares, but the numbers were not adding up for him. He was supposed to have at least 20% from this US company, but in reality, he had less than a percent. On top of his shares being diluted, his patches, Nutriband's product, were shelved by the company so they could sit on the technology.

I could not help but see my younger self in Gareth, trying to navigate this world of business with little experience and dishonest figures trying to take advantage of him. With all of my nightmare scenarios with Tedrow and the Asconi lawsuit right when I was hitting thirty, I knew he had a treacherous road ahead of him. I made it clear to Gareth that I would act in the capacity of a consultant, and together, we would write a letter to the CEO of the company that acquired Nutriband. The goal of the letter was to ask for a rescission of the contract. I designed the letter using as serious legal terms as I could to make it clear to the CEO that we meant business. To our surprise, the CEO agreed to rescind the deal immediately, and it was time to get to work.

We formed Nutriband USA as a Nevada corporation, and at the beginning, I had a smaller percentage in the company because I was just a consultant in the deal. Gareth and I found we needed to raise more money and land a big investment, so I reached out to my friend from law school, Vitalie Botgros, who had his own charter plane company. We struck a deal where Gareth gave back five million shares to the treasury, so half of the company was Gareth's and the other half was split between my friend and me. If I was Thomas Tedrow, Gareth would have only gotten 5%, but I'm not Thomas.

Nutriband's first Board of Directors.: Vitalie Botgros (right), Gareth Sheridan (center) and I (left). Together, we are the three pieces that made Nutriband happen.

I knew Gareth was the creative driving force behind everything Nutriband was doing, and it was his imagination that would bring real success to the company. That in and of itself required we hold the largest share in the company.

We made the company official on January 4, 2016, and we filed a Form 10 with the SEC a few months later to make it a public company. We even started looking into acquiring a company, Advanced Health, for their IP, and during the negotiations, we were put in touch with their lawyer that had FDA experience. Advanced Health's lawyer was more than willing to help us and provided us with a very extensive and detailed opinion that we did not need FDA approval in the US. We also had a range of doctors and a dermatologist advising us on Nutriband's product, and the consensus was that these patches could be called vitamin patches and would fall under the category of supplements.

Once we started filing our official financials, we received an invitation for an interview with the SEC, which I was slightly concerned about, especially with my experience with the SEC from my Asconi days. We had not been subpoenaed and it was an informal interview, but I was at a loss for why they would want to talk to us. We did not have trading stock and still needed to go through FINRA to get a stock symbol. We were at least six to twelve months away from our first trade on the stock, but the only concern I had was on the FDA disclosure.

After reassuring myself with the written opinion from Advanced Health's legal counsel, presented to us as an FDA lawyer, I went to the interview in Miami without a lawyer; I felt quite comfortable with where the company stood.

There were two interviewers: an American guy who was quite amiable and a French or Belgian guy who was not afraid to raise his voice at me. The two of them began to pressure me right away, specifically wanting information on Gareth and any potential misdoings, but all I had to say about Gareth was positive. They asked me how much money we had in the account for the company, and I could remember exactly how much was in the account: $40. After about three or four hours, the French/Belgian interviewer was raising his voice at me, and we were soon in a screaming match. Since it was an informal interview and I didn't have a lawyer with me, I eventually left, but I knew Gareth would be next.

We got Gareth a lawyer for his interview, and at this point, we still did not know what the SEC was hunting for. After Gareth's interview did not reveal any purposeful misdoings, they raised our informal interviews to a formal investigation. They went to the lawyer who first gave us the opinion that we didn't need FDA approval from Advanced Health, the company we acquired (or so we thought) for five million shares of Nutriband stock, and she immediately tried to throw us under the bus.

First, she lied and initially said she never gave us an opinion, but of course, we had printed out copies of her emails. Then, she told the SEC that she misunderstood what the opinion was for, but that was a lie as well. We provided the SEC with all of our documents because we knew we were in the right, but it still did not matter. We were scrambling.

In retrospect, I feel slightly ashamed of how cocky I behaved during that initial interview. If only I could have known that the FDA opinion I was basing myself on was a bad, inaccurate opinion that I never should have been relied upon.

Around June of 2017, everything was going wrong with the SEC investigation, and FINRA was slow in responding to comments; it looked like there was no end in sight for when we would be receiving the symbol. I did what I always do in those types of situations: pray and turn things over to a higher power.

I called Gareth, telling him, "Partner, we've hit a roadblock. It's a big one. Unless we get a symbol soon, I don't know if we'll be able to survive." I laid out my Hail Mary: we would both give away 100,000 shares to our churches. I am Christian Orthodox, and Gareth is Irish Catholic. The very next day after I shared my pledge with Gareth, we received a notification from our market maker sponsor: FINRA had approved our application and granted us the symbol NTRB! We had not even called the transfer agent yet, but our prayer was heard. We transferred the shares as we had planned, ready for what came next.

In 2018, our lawyer told us that the SEC was preparing to send us a Wells Notice, meaning they were preparing to sue us, and it couldn't have been at a worse time. The stock was just starting to take off and was trading at around $9. We were also about to have our first major shareholder meeting to elect the new board of directors when we found out the parties in the Advanced Health deal had committed fraud. While we prepared our lawsuit against those involved at Advanced Health, the SEC came to us with a settlement: Gareth and I were to each pay $75,000 and resign from the board, effectively killing the company and instating a ban that would prohibit us from ever being on the board of a company.

I met with Gareth and told him we had to be on the same page. If we took the settlement, we would never be able to work in this business again, and we'd have to start looking for jobs at a car wash. We knew we had to fight, and there was even a good chance we were going to win; when they initially interviewed us, we only had $40 in the account, but now we had over $1 million in the account. We got to work right away.

Gareth and I started by going to a large FDA law firm and spent $7000 to get a proper opinion on Nutriband's product in relation to the FDA. The firm explained to us that we needed to be approved by the FDA, and the opinion we had gotten before was not correct.

The SEC told us in the investigation that they had an opinion from the FDA, which is why they were emboldened to send us a Wells Notice, but we were never shown proof of that opinion. This is most likely because the FDA does not directly issue opinions, or at least that we were led to believe, and we came to realize that the SEC was possibly bluffing and didn't even have an opinion. At the end of the day though, we still needed FDA approval for vitamin patches, which could take millions of dollars and many years in FDA trials.

After consulting with the FDA lawyers, we went to Joe Dever, a lawyer who had experience as a former enforcement attorney with the SEC at Cozen O'Connor in New York. He saw that we had a case and approached the SEC, noting a very detailed letter of explanation of our position, the reasoning, and the basis for our filings, implying that we were ready to fight back. We responded to the Wells Notice, and after that, the SEC took a step back. The threats of fraud and never being on a board again disappeared, but we were still hit with a slap on the wrist which later proved to be a painful one.

Without admitting or denying any guilt, we agreed to cease and desist from committing or causing any violations and any future violations of Exchange Act Sections 12(g) and 13(a) and Rules 12b-20 and 13a-1, paying the $25,000 fine for making the mistake in the filings. We were free to continue to work, raise money, and never be considered a bad actor; however, this investigation would come back to haunt us when we applied to NASDAQ.

Nutriband was growing with great success, the stock was trading at $25, and there was general interest in investing in us. We were sure that we would make it onto the NASDAQ and continue the company's success. With that confidence, we applied in 2020.

Before we heard back, I had a dream that I was walking up a flight of stairs to a shabby room, very similar to the dorms from law school in Moldova. Inside, Gareth was talking on the phone with NASDAQ, and what they were talking about sounded controversial. Despite this, I suddenly felt exuberantly happy, weeping with tears: we had gotten onto NASDAQ. Once I woke up, I told Gareth and some investors about my dream, only to be completely disappointed just two weeks later.

We were denied, most likely because we were too small of a company at the time. The SEC settlement on our record did not look good, and we were told that we would have to step down as directors if we wanted the company to move forward. Gareth and I grudgingly accepted this and told the team at NASDAQ that we would step down and name someone else.

In October of 2019, just before the gymnastics of trying to secure NASDAQ approval, we had just taken a convertible debenture on the advice of our bankers, which, in my 20 years of building businesses, I had never advised anyone to do. We were told by our bankers who'd recommended the deal we'd be on NASDAQ in thirty days, so this would show the market we were able to raise money.

The convertible debenture ate all of our equity; not one share of stock was converted, and we were sitting on debt we had to pay off. It's possible that the bank was shorting us as we were initially trading around $25, but when NASDAQ denied us, it was at $12.

Gareth and I were paying with our own resources to have a suite at the Orlando Magic's basketball arena for meetings, even though we didn't have much money at the time. After we got the notice from NASDAQ, Gareth and I decided to go to a game, just the two of us. We put our heads together and realized we had been relying on consultants this whole time, for over 12 months. Everybody was consulting us, but we were the ones who had the most to lose in these situations. We realized we could either withdraw our application and boost up our numbers, or we could fight.

If we chose to fight, we would need to inform the market through an official SEC filing that NASDAQ had denied our application and file for an appeal. That would mean that the whole market could find out, but we were more worried about our convertible debenture and the actors behind those funds.

If the bank found out about our application withdrawal, they would, in the most likely scenario, immediately convert all of their loan into stock, pushing the price to a penny stock. If they were shorting our stock, they would profit while we would flounder. This scenario was unacceptable, and after, I confirmed with the American Stock Transfer that not one share had been converted yet on the convertible debenture. Then, we went to work on the deal that would save the company and give it a chance to see another day.

We invited a couple of family money managers and small family brokers to our suite at a basketball game. We had a pitch for a small private placement. In mid-February 2019 when we got out of the game—I don't even recall who was playing—we had a commitment for a $700,000 raise. As soon as the raise was completed, we paid off the convertible debenture in full before they were able to convert into one share of Nutriband Inc. stock. We withdrew our application from NASDAQ, and we were told that we could reapply 12 months later. About one week after we withdrew the application, the COVID pandemic started, and that NASDAQ denial now looked like a blessing in disguise.

Our new plan was to restructure the business and apply to NASDAQ a year later. As part of the restructuring and strengthening of the shareholders' equity and balance sheet, we went after the acquisition of Pocono Coated Products for $6 million in company stock and a $1.5 million promissory note. Exactly 12 months and a couple of days after withdrawing our application, we submitted the NASDAQ application again.

When Gareth and I applied that second time, we worked with the same analyst as last time, who was quite impressed with how far we had come. When we first applied in 2019, we had roughly $700,000 in shareholder equity and almost no assets. When we next applied, we had $7.5 million in shareholder equity and about $10 million in assets. Nutriband's sales in the Korean market had hit about half a million dollars in sales, and overall, the company was looking great. We even hired Donohoe Advisory Associates, a consulting firm that was led by the former chief counsel for the NASDAQ, to make sure we had additional help.

Suddenly, our analyst, who knew our case from our initial filing a year before, decided to move on from NASDAQ. Before he left, he told us that we were in the last stage before we would be accepted, but for the next few months, we sat in limbo and had no news. I eventually got a call from Gareth, and I could hear the panic in his voice as he told me that we had been denied again. I calmed down Gareth and told him there was only one option ahead of us: we had to fight.

I wrote an impassioned letter and explained that we were going to file an appeal, stating they would have to explain why we were being denied and why Gareth and I were not allowed to be on the board of directors. I based my opinion on the assumption that the NASDAQ analysts were simply overwhelmed by the quantity of work after coming off of the Covid-19 lockdowns. In this case, it would make sense to overlook or make a rush decision on a case that has been denied already once before. The appeal wouldn't be handled by NASDAQ either; it would go to two independent business people, so NASDAQ would have to explain to them why we were being denied.

At this point in the process, I had quit my CFO position in Nutriband to appease NASDAQ, remaining just a director, and I found myself wanting to focus on family again.

In August of 2021, my dad was turning 75 years old, and it was always his dream to see the Grand Canyon. He had grown up reading about Indians and cowboys of the Wild West, and I wanted to make this dream of his come true. In the past, we had planned trips to go, but something always got in the way. One time, I tore my Achilles heel playing soccer just before we were about to go, and we had to cancel the trip. This time, it worked out for us, so I took my father and my nephew to the Grand Canyon, and we popped champagne at midnight to toast my father's 75th birthday.

Our trip ended in Las Vegas, so my nephew, my father, and I had plenty of fun where we stayed at the Luxor Hotel. On the morning of August 23, 2021, my dad's birthday, we were sitting around the pool when I got a call from Gareth: the business board had reversed the NASDAQ denial. I excused myself from my dad and nephew, keeping this information to myself, and went back to the room. From the window, I had the same view of Las Vegas as I did when I first met Gareth on Thanksgiving of 2015. I fell to my knees and wept for about 10 minutes straight, just like in the dream I saw about 18 months before.

After the initial shock and exuberance left my body, I returned to the pool, without saying a word to my dad or my nephew, exemplifying another rule that I marked for myself a long time ago. I do not share any information, good or bad, with my family until it becomes public. When I applied for the position of the Governor of the Central Bank of Moldova, everyone, including my parents, found out from the official news, same with my Air Moldova transaction, same as now. This might be due to the fact that I am extremely superstitious. With bad news, you can magnify the effect and create unnecessary pressure on those close to you. With bad news, they will be worried without being able to help with anything; with good news, you might just jinx it. Either way, we had a marvelous birthday celebration for my dad that day, partying into the early hours of the morning!

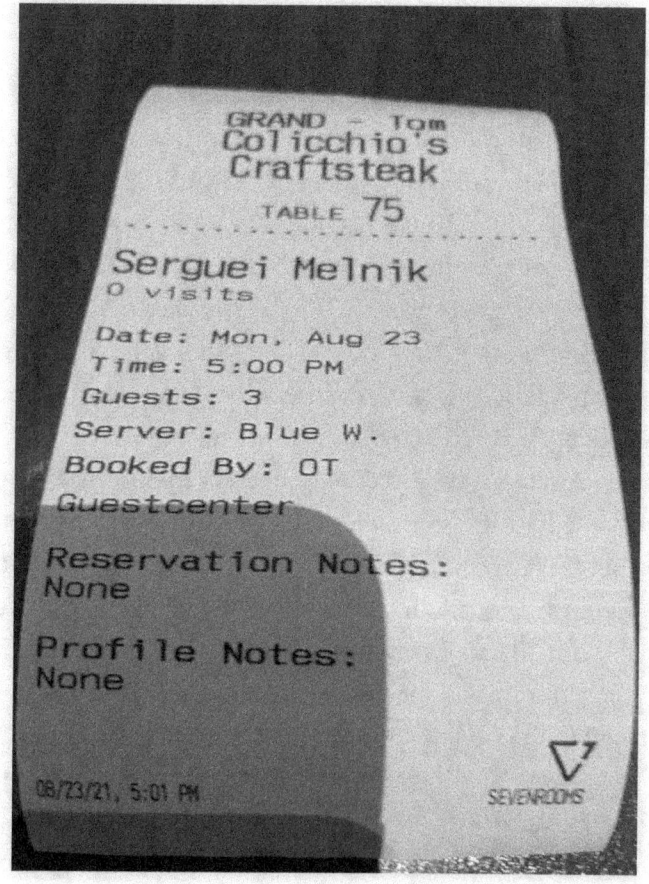

I believe a lot in fate, this is the restaurant reservation and the table number on the day of my Dad's Birthday, my Dad turned 75...

THE ROAD TO KILIMANJARO

Father and son, strolling through Vegas, on 23rd of August, 2021.

I made my Dad's dream come true. Grand Canyon.

About a month later, Nutriband received official approval, and on October 1, 2021, we were a NASDAQ company. Our IPO was initiated, we raised about $6 million, and about two weeks later, I was offered the president's position. It was a series of real fights, but when considering what drove me through the hardships, it always came back to my relationship with Gareth and how much I believed in the work he was doing.

Nutriband's battles aren't over, but we know where we stand in our fights: no matter what anyone throws at us, we know we are doing the right thing.

October 1, 2023. Nutriband IPO was listed on NASDAQ.
I celebrated with my family and friends.

Gareth and I sharing cigars and cognac to celebrate Nutriband's listing. The cognac, Suvorov, was 40 years old aged. I purchased it with my earliest earnings in fall of 1999. I made $15,000 on a transaction with Vadim Enikeev. I bought two bottles: one I drank right away with my Dad, the other bottle I kept for a special occasion. That special occasion came 22 years later. Gareth was barely 10 years old when I bought that cognac.

CHAPTER 8:

Nutriband's Future, My Future

————•————

Reporting on our second quarter in 2022, we were about two weeks shy from October 1, our one-year anniversary of trading on NASDAQ. Our cash position is still strong, and even though we chose to fend off any dilutive fundraising offers, our second quarter revenue just grew over 100% when compared to our second quarter of 2021. We feel we are on the right track, and the partnership with Kindeva is going as we planned. We have traveled a long way from February of 2020, the pre-pandemic time when we were first denied entry into the exclusive club of companies trading on NASDAQ.

We're growing in our capacity to tackle real problems and make real change. Currently, we're embarking on a joint venture with a successful pharmaceutical company. The factory in North Carolina has the capacity to manufacture one million patches in just 24 hours. Our focus is to create abuse-deterrent transdermal patches, such as fentanyl transdermal patches with an extended release for the treatment of chronic pain.

December 3, 2021, family showed up to support Nutriband on its Ringing of the Opening Bell on NASDAQ

Gareth and I, founders of Nutriband Inc., after ringing the Opening Bell in front of NASDAQ in Times Square, New York.

The patch technology can be adapted to almost any transdermal patch on the market today *without* the risk of abuse or misuse. It's radical science that could change the lives of millions. The idea is to establish a new safety standard for transdermal opioids, but the opportunity for this technology is not limited solely to opioids. In our research, we have noted many more products that could benefit from this technology, even, for example, the prevention of accidental misuse in children or choking hazards.

With the growth we've enjoyed so far, there have still been ongoing struggles. Our first ever acquisition, that of Advanced Health, an Ohio-based company, started around the same time as the SEC became interested in us. Gareth saw potential in their IP (I don't understand all of it, but that is why I have Gareth), and we bought them for five million shares around May of 2017, which cost 25% of Nutriband.

Advanced Health came in with their CFO, Laura Fillman, and their lawyer, Michelle Polly-Murphy; it would eventually be Michelle who gave us the opinion that I presented to the SEC to show them that our products do not need FDA registration.

All through the SEC investigation and for subsequent 2017 and 2018 filings, we entirely relied on her opinion in our disclosures and arguments with the SEC. By January 2018, we were trading, finally, and had two quarters on file when the auditors struck down our purchase price of $2.5 million to zero. They felt that Advanced Health was not worth anything, which left Gareth and I taken aback. There was an asterisk, indicating the price could be revised in the future, but we had no idea what was going on as we were partway through our first roadshow, meeting with a range of bankers.

During the roadshow, I received a request to remove the restriction legend in order to sell 100,000 shares from someone called John Baker. Now, I did not recall who that was, so I called Gareth to learn more about John Baker as nobody besides us, and perhaps some of our family members and original investors, had such large stock positions in the company.

We learned that he was part of the Ohio deal with Advanced Health, which meant he would be considered an insider. As insiders, like Gareth and me, they couldn't sell shares like this; we approached the shareholders to sign a lock-up agreement. These are fairly rudimentary, so when we first approached the CFO, Laura Feldman, she agreed right away—a sign that she was the only decent person in the company. When we approached the lawyer, Michelle Polly-Murphy, she refused to sign, and then everybody else followed her lead and refused as well. We could feel that something very strange was going on.

At the same time, Gareth called me with a problem: when he checked the IP from Advanced Health, it came up under Raymond Kalmar's name, one of the main shareholders of Advanced Health, the company we had purchased. The IP was still supposed to be under Advanced Health, which we owned, so we challenged the lawyer.

She told us that a transfer like this can happen right away; it was not that easy though as I made my point in the follow-up email to her and Kalmar. We were making certain disclosures with the SEC and Advanced Health's IP. To see Ray Kalmar's name pop up as the owner of the IP, long after we purchased Advanced Health, was a red flag, so we hired a third-party law firm to investigate what exactly was happening. A month later, we finally got a clearer picture of what was going on: this team at Advanced Health had dissolved the company back in January without telling us. It was a huge mess as it was a distinct event that we had to disclose to shareholders through the 8-K form at the time of dissolution. Then, Raymond Kalmar put the IP in his name, so he could benefit from Nutriband's stocks and still hold onto the IP, all without telling us anything. We'd been outmaneuvered.

We also had a background check run on Kalmar, and it came with a lengthy record of dishonest crimes across three states, a conviction for writing a bad check, and two bankruptcies. Kalmar also claimed to be the founder of a veteran charity foundation, and yet, we could not find any record of it. Kalmar maintains he'd served two tours in Iraq, which he proudly announced during the subsequent court hearings. The only problem with that: records show Kalmar was in the US Air Force between 1983 to 1995. There were no US troops stationed in Iraq during that period, so unless he toured Iraq as a tourist, it would not have been possible.

Kalmar most likely preyed upon people's poor understanding of history and the memories of the first Gulf War, Operation Desert Storm, but I did not fall for it. I love history, and those events happened during my freshman year in law school at the Moldova State University when I had aspirations to be a diplomat. I remember that time in definitive detail, including how many people the allied forces lost and what the UN Security Council mandate was for the liberation of Kuwait. The USSR was still alive then, and the mandate for the security council was very definite: liberate Kuwait, and do not advance into Iraq territory. This is exactly what was achieved, and lying about such a sensitive topic, especially in the light of the later Iraq war and thousands of US casualties, just seemed particularly sinister of Kalmar.

To make matters worse, Kalmar and another former Advanced Health member were appointed to the board of directors of Nutriband Inc. after our acquisition. I knew we needed to remedy this quickly. First, we had to call in the shareholders for a meeting in July of 2018, and as soon as the meeting was over and the new board was elected, a same-day resolution was passed to rescind the Advanced Health deal and engage the law firm to file a lawsuit to recover the Nutriband stock issued to Kalmar and company.

We responded as quickly as possible, filing an 8-K to the SEC, rescinding the deal, and filing a lawsuit to recover the 25% of Nutriband that they took in exchange for the acquisition.

Gareth and I interacted quite often with Michelle Polly-Murphy when we were signing the deal initially with Advanced Health, and she handled things with a sense that "everything was fine." As we found out that everything was indeed *not* fine, we filed a complaint against her. She was subsequently fired from her law firm, then suspended by the Ohio State Bar Association.

For the past four years, this team from Advanced Health has traded the Nutriband stocks for collateral—about $300,000 worth—with a finance firm to fight our lawsuit.

On the very first injunction hearing, presided over by retiring Judge Rodriguez, everything that could have gone wrong *did* go wrong. I could see right away that Judge

Rodriguez was not particularly interested in the details of the case; he was, however, very impressed by Kalmar's two "tours" in Iraq. To Rodriguez, it did not seem to matter that Kalmar and the company did not transfer the stock into the escrow as he requested, though we did put in our $50,000. At one point during the hearing, our lawyers pointed this to Rodriguez, only for him to respond, "I am comfortable where the stock is now," whatever that was supposed to mean in legal terms.

It was a strange hearing, especially when you could see the judge talk more than the opposing parties, constantly interfering in the process. At the same time, Rodriguez was slobbering all over his much younger and beautiful clerk, paying her compliments and telling the court how much he envied the next judge who would have the chance to work with her as he was retiring and this was his last case. It was all hard to watch.

I felt our lawyers' performance at that time was toothless since the opposing counsel was having a field day with them, directly insulting myself and Gareth multiple times without any repercussions from our lawyers or the judge. When our lawyers brought in the record of Kalmar's dishonest crimes, I happened to make eye contact with Judge Rodriguez, and boy, he did not like that!

He threw me out of the courtroom for making eye contact with him... Funny thing is that psychologically, it all made perfect sense. I remembered the quote from Carl Sagan: "One of the saddest lessons of history is this: if we've been bamboozled long enough, we tend to reject any evidence of the bamboozle. We are not interested in finding out the truth. The bamboozle has captured us. It's simply too painful to acknowledge. Once you give a charlatan power over you, you almost never get it back."

This judge believed the lies and couldn't see them for what they were. My instincts were correct, and the judge's verdict made no logical sense: he dissolved the injunction, decided to leave the stock with Kalmar and the company, and gave them our $50,000, all while requiring them to issue the IP (that we did not want anymore) in Nutriband Inc.'s name.

Long story short, our lawyers, who I was so unhappy with after the first hearing, appealed and reversed the verdict about one year later. On June 27, 2022, almost exactly four years after we discovered the fraud purported on our company and its shareholders, we got our day in court, and this time, the new judge was almost invisible in the room, letting the parties expose all of the facts and being attentive to every detail presented in the case.

In that courtroom, I finally saw our chief litigator, Jay Brennan, giving his best performance; I wish the process was recorded so we could rewind and see the amazing litigation skill he presented. He never raised his voice, but every argument or rebuff that he made just shredded through the opposing counsel's rhetoric. I had invited my nephew, Sergio, to the hearing. He had just graduated from UF with a master's in entrepreneurship and was accepted to attend Wake Forest University School of Law as a freshman that fall. Seeing the masterclass performance by Jay Brennan, who has practiced law for 42 years, might just have convinced Sergio to go into litigation instead of his originally planned corporate transactional law. I knew he would gain a lot from this experience, even if I would have preferred that this hiccup hadn't happened at all. Nutriband came out the other side though, and I'm immensely proud of how far both Gareth and I have come.

All throughout this lawsuit, I've continued to see my younger self in Gareth, with bad actors trying to take advantage of him at every opportunity. He has an honest heart, and he's so hardworking. It's been a joy to work beside him all of these years.

I'm glad I had as much experience in dealing with other businesspeople, like Ray Kalmar, and that I could be a part of Nutriband to help Gareth through this incredibly difficult time. We knew we couldn't just give up and leave part of Nutriband in the hands of these morally-bankrupt people, nor could we allow them to keep a hold of even one share of Nutriband stock.

As of July 2022, our fortitude in the case paid off; it was a landslide win on absolutely all counts. My only regret is that I did not see the chief opposing counsel's face when he read the verdict.

Ray Kalmar won nothing, and now they are returning 1.2 million shares, worth about 15% of the company, to all Nutriband shareholders. We have Jay Brennan and our lawyers from Gray Robinson to thank for this, but it helps knowing that we were persistent in proving Kalmar's nefarious behavior. After the final verdict was official, the opposing counsel contacted us with a settlement offer: they would accept the final judgment and not file an appeal as long as Nutriband did not go after them for our legal and other damages, such as the $50,000 "gifted" to them by Judge

Rodriguez. I wanted to scorch Kalmar and his party, but at the end of the day, once we win over all the damages and legal fees, who would we collect them from?

This battle was over; we won fair and square. We rewarded every shareholder with the exact percentage of stock that we returned from the lawsuit, and we achieved everything we set out to achieve.

Before Nutriband's IPO, I had a dream where I saw a beautiful SUV sitting in a parking lot, and somehow, I inherently knew it was mine. I naturally pulled open the door and sat in the driver's seat, but to my surprise, the steering wheel wasn't in front of me. It was in the middle, between the driver and passenger seat. Afterwards, I told Gareth about my dream; I knew it was a sign that he and I were to drive Nutriband forward together. It also makes perfect sense that I sat in the driver's seat on the left and Gareth, who is from Ireland, sat on the right—which is the side they have the steering wheel on. Together, we have been able to support Nutriband through rough times, and our success is due to us trusting one another and ourselves over the promises of other people.

Now, Nutriband's future looks bright: we're opening a new market in Costa Rica, opening a company in Ecuador as well, and the factory in North Carolina has the capacity to produce one million patches in a day.

Nutriband has also been working with Kindeva Drug Delivery to develop our AVERSA abuse-deterrent technology into their fentanyl patches. We're looking to scale up and give Nutriband the growth that it needs to become a $1,000 stock; this will be our next summit to conquer. It will continue to be a fight, but I know we won't be dissuaded by anyone.

The road leading to this point seemed impossible, but our resilience and determination has only been reinforced by these great successes. If you are going to dream, you might as well dream big. Do not limit your expectations.

I often stop to think about my own future as well. Through all of this, from my days in Moldova to Nutriband, I fought so hard for what I believed is the right thing, and even with all of those hard fights, I still feel that my biggest accomplishments are my children.

I have a true sense of self from building a relationship with them, particularly in ways that my father never did with me. I see it when I constantly quiz my children while I drive them to school. I have a deep love for classical music, and as pieces come on the radio, I have them tell me the names of each. Korsakov's "Flight of the Bumblebee" recently played, and I immediately quizzed my son. "It's Bumblebee, dad," my son groaned as if it was too easy.

Another day, my daughter was playing a game when Grieg's "Morning Mood" began to play, to which she exclaimed, "Morning Mood!" once she recognized the piece. Eventually, my kids will tire of me quizzing them all of the time, but I hope they will appreciate this knowledge later on because classical music is a part of my everyday life balance, and I want to pass it down to them.

Before 1986, my exposure to classical music was limited to watching and listening to it on the TV, particularly whenever a Communist Party Leader would die, they would play classical music concerts on the State TV for three days straight. We had just two TV channels, both playing the same (to my mind) awful music and an absolute lack of entertaining programs for those days. I would absolutely hate it! My love for classical music was awoken in the summer of 1986 at Sergeevka Pioneer (Boy Scout) Campus located in Ukraine by the Black Sea. My parents sent me and my sister to Sergeevka for the summer to shield us from the legal battles my Dad was facing at home. My sister and I were separated by age and gender and we were placed in units with our peers.

One beautiful south Ukraine summer day one kid, who was considered the bad boy and trouble maker of our 14 Under unit (always getting in trouble and always one step away from his parents being called to the Camp to pick him up and take him home), found an accordion in the supervisor's office. The boy's last name was Musulbas, which is a very non Moldovan or Russian name, which I have never heard before or after I met him. Maybe that was the reason that I still remember that name. Musulbas quickly picked up the accordion, sat down, and gave the most astonishing performance of a classical music piece that I have ever heard. He interpreted the Turkish March by Mozart and he was overheard by the supervisor himself, who when entered the room was in visible shock to see what the "Bad Boy" was capable of. The Turkish March became the song of our Unit, where we 30 boys would march together and would hum in unison, from the first to the last note. We even took first place in the March and Sing contest among all the units at the Camp. I don't think I had ever heard a classical music interpretation of a piece from the beginning to the end before Musulbas picked up that accordion in 1986 in Sergeevka. Bad Boy Musulbas inspired my love for classical music from then on.

MAny years ago, before we had kids, I was playing soccer for a Mexican team in the Central Florida amateurs league. During one of the weekly practices we were playing a scrimmage and the owners of the team invited their teenaged kids to play with us. I quickly realized that their English was very poor with a strong accent so I switched to Spanish to communicate with them. To my absolute horror, the kids could not speak Spanish, they were speaking English exactly like their parents, even though they were born in the US. When I got home that night I asked Jazmina to promise me that when we have kids we will never speak English at home with them and that is exactly what we followed, since the moment our kids were born that would hear just Spanish from their Mother and just Romanian from their Dad. When Dmitry went to school at 5 years old, he did not speak a word of English, but he was fluent in Romanian and Spanish. ITs not easy to maintain this rule once the kids grow up, but we try our best.Today both of our kids are fluent in three languages.

Even with this knowledge, I know there is an important lesson in keeping dreams alive as a child. About three years ago, when my son, Dmitry, was nine, he returned from school and began questioning the existence of Santa Claus. Unsure of what he had heard from his friends at school, he shyly asked me if Santa was real. I told him, "How about this Christmas, we fly to the North Pole to visit Santa?" I immediately had a flash back of when I got the shocking news that Santa was not real. It was from Arthur Scripnic, my classmate, and I was 7 years old. I remember coming home and asking Mom and her answer was not clear at all what made me understand that Arthur was right.

Refusing to accept the natural flow of such events so soon, I immediately made the arrangements, and on Christmas Day of 2019, we flew to Rovaniemi, Lapland to visit Santa Claus. The children had a blast, and we stayed in Finland until January 3, skiing, riding with reindeers, and having a magical New Year's celebration at an old goldmine. I did my best to provide the most inspiring Christmas vacation to my kids. After we saw Santa Claus, I asked Dmitry, "So, if anyone ever doubts his existence, what do you tell them?"

"I will tell them to just go and see for themselves," said Dmitry.

This is behavior my parents would have never attempted for my sister or me. Compared to how busy my father was when I was a child, my children are a priority when it comes to dividing my time.

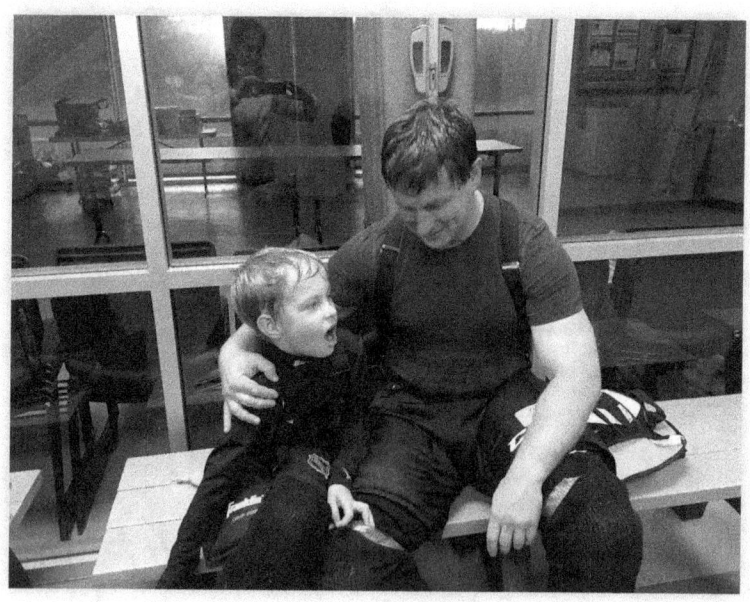

Back when I could keep up with my son on the ice.

From the day that I just could not miss.I was lucky
to take my Princess on the ice for the first time.

Meeting Santa Claus!

I once had a very important meeting in Moldova, arranging the acquisition of the largest airline company in the country, Air Moldova. With the publicity I had gotten from applying to be the head of the Central Bank of Moldova, I was able to get a good deal based on the fact that I would bring them public to the US financial markets. At that time, I had already identified for them a NASDAQ SPAC (special purpose acquisition company) with $100,000,000 and another $200,000,000 in bonds to be issued.

The SPAC was excited with the preliminary numbers that I sent them, and all that remained was to receive the real numbers from an audit company. Unfortunately, the financial balance sheet after privatization showed a total mess: there was a significant number of records missing all of the way back to 2014. It was increasingly clear that the auditing of Air Moldova would not be a several-months event, but rather a couple of years. Also, a year after the privatization, the political atmosphere changed, throwing the whole deal in limbo.

During that Air Moldova meeting in August of 2018, I had to stay longer for the deal to happen, but that particular weekend, I knew I just had to be in Orlando since my daughter was about to get on ice for the very first time. It was a Thursday, and I told my client's legal representative that missing such a moment was not an option, so they flew me out of Moldova on a Friday morning, and Saturday morning, I was with my daughter at the skating rink. On Sunday, I flew back to Moldova, and I was back in the office in Chisinau on Monday afternoon. It was a whirlwind, but experiencing that first moment of skating with my daughter was worth all of the travel and jet lag. I can still picture her smile and joy from that day.

I also rarely miss my son's hockey games as it was my dream to watch him skate and play hockey. Growing up, there was not one ice rink in all of Moldova. As children, we would skate on the frozen lakes when we could during the winter, but to play hockey more seriously would have been a dream come true. Now, my son can skate to his heart's content, and I know I have given him opportunities I never had as a child.

With Nutriband still one of my main priorities, Gareth has seen how important my children are to me, and I've told him that they are my future. Gareth is younger than I am and doesn't have children yet, but I made sure to give him advice I truly believe in: "You're going to get accustomed to business success and to a much larger checking account, but this overwhelming joy of success will eventually dwindle.

You are just going to get used to being rich, but every day and night with your kids, you'll wake up to that joy that never goes away. My children. They make me feel full."

I look at my career, building companies up, taking them to NASDAQ, and I am pleased with my work, but when I look at my children, I feel light—I feel complete.

Conclusion

There is a Russian saying on judging how a man lives his life: "A man is characterized by four situations: how he fights, how he counts money, how he looks at his children, and how he leaves a woman."

I've always been a fighter. I began by taking this principle quite literally, becoming a judo and wrestling champion in my teens, second degree black belt in my thirties, and a jiu-jitsu wrestler in my forties. I've had physical matches and brawls guide my fate, but there is an aspect of the spirit of the fight that runs through life itself. Whether it be fighting for a spot for my son on a travel hockey team that is plagued by nepotism from the coaches and even small local government officials (who are mostly irrelevant in the public service, but "powerful" on the hockey travel team board of directors) or the legal battle against Advanced Health to recuperate the 15% of our company, to look yourself in the mirror afterwards and see that you were true to your principles is often the real victory. Every fight leaves a scar you will carry through the rest of your life, but it's a marker of experience and a reminder that you live to fight another day.

Everyone fights for different reasons though, and many fight to hoard as much money they can get their hands on. I've met many men and women who are driven by the belief that they do not have enough and never will. I put my trust in these people and was repeatedly treated as if I were merely an obstacle in the way of their next big deal when I could have been an ally. Having also befriended honest business people, such as Gareth, I've been able to hone my ability to spot the people who are going to use you for their own benefit. If I could give my children any advice, it would be to never befriend greedy people; those with only money on their mind will betray you or sell you for next to nothing, often at the most inopportune time. I've learned to take money very seriously, but even still, money itself can never be the target; it's just a means, a tool, an energy. Whoever believes that money can somehow summon happiness has never truly had money. I never want my children to experience the shortages I've had in my life. My wife is worried that our kids do not really understand the value of money, but the fact that they can grow separately from those kinds of thoughts and worries makes me feel extremely accomplished.

We traveled to Ecuador, accompanied by family and friends, to celebrate our 25th year Wedding Anniversary at exactly the same venue when we got married in December of 1996.

The same Groom and Bride, the same country, the same city and the same venue, even the same tuxedo for the Groom (small alterations later on) ... only 25 years before, December 21, 1996.

Silver Wedding, December 17, 2021

The Centers of my Universe.

My children are the absolute center of my universe, constantly pulling me towards greater happiness with their love and own passion for life. The entirety of my work schedule is built around piano lessons, skating, hockey, and any other events in my kids' lives. This has been the case since they were born, and I hope to keep it this way as long as I can, with my family being what makes me complete. If anyone should look at me, they will see that I am in the exact place in life where I want to be; I am lucky enough to have everything I could ever ask for. There are many times that I find myself thinking of how I would react as a child if I had a glimpse of myself in the future, nowadays… I am pretty sure I would say: "old man, looks we did allright"... My son and my daughter are the two brightest points of light in my life, and they will guide me until the end.

Now when it comes to the final aspect of the Russian quote, how a man "leaves a woman," I am lucky to not have much experience in that regard. I have had girlfriends as a young man, but my relationship with Jazmina is a collaborative and passionate marriage built on trust, understanding, and communication. Personally, I hope to never learn more about leaving a woman in that traditional sense; though, I will say I have felt loss when leaving behind someone I cared very deeply for: my grandmother.

I often think about my grandparent's farm and that key memory of waking up and seeing the sun stream in with the wind blowing through the house's open windows. Listening to my grandparents setting up a breakfast of fresh fruit and bread, I felt such a calmness that continues to resonate in me even now. My family spent every summer at that farmhouse, and because of that, I have memories of us coming together, which many families do not have.

My grandmother's death was particularly painful for me; she raised me until I was three and was a true matriarch leading the family. In May of 1995, we had gathered the whole family together to meet Jazmina for the first time and to see me after being away overseas for a year. It was the last time the family was ever together like this, and we were lucky enough to have pictures and videos from this gathering. All of these years later, I remember when I got the phone call from my sister that my grandmother had passed, the pain shot through my heart as I felt an immeasurable loss.

In June of 199, Jazmina was able to meet my family in Moldova., including my grandparents. The car in the picture, a Gaz 69, was assembled by my Grandpa himself. The car was inherited by my cousin Viorel, who I later purchased the car from. The only thing I changed in the car was the engine, but the rest are all original parts that my Grandpa installed. Everytime I get in the car, the smell of it, the touch throws me back into my childhood at the farm.

The first thing that came to mind after that call was a memory I had of my grandmother dressing me when I was just three years old. She said, "You're a kid right now, but then you're going to grow up."

"Yes," I replied.

"And then like everybody, you'll get old," my grandma said.

"Yes," I said, "and then I'm gonna get born again."

"No," she told me. "Unfortunately, then you die."

Of course, I didn't understand what death was, but now that it's years later, I have a better understanding of that step in life. It's painful and sad, yet it is not the end. Everything doesn't just stop; it keeps going.

Everything that happened after my sister's call about my grandma was so easy: somehow, everyone was able to get to Moldova quickly with no trouble at all. My parents just happened to be getting on a connecting flight in Hungary to the United States, so they were allowed off the plane to get to Moldova. I got a ticket right away, my flight had no delays, and my family was able to come together at a time when we needed it the most.

After both my grandparents passed away, my uncle wanted to sell the same farmhouse that I had all of these great memories of. I made a deal with my uncle so that the farm and the house became mine, even though nobody will live there. It will remain in the family, and it can be a place where I share memories with my own children and future generations.

Of course, I would like to have my grandma alive, but that is just not how life works. Life continues on, and no matter the hardships, I had to live my life and do my work.

I don't hold regret for the past; I wake up every morning with joy for the day and dreams of my future. A negative result is still a result; mistakes are simply attempts to learn to do better next time.

Good things don't just happen to you; that is not what makes you happy. You have to work hard for everything you want to achieve, and then, in the gratitude and fulfillment of your work, you can actually find happiness. Whatever bad things that have happened in your past, you must overcome because maybe they happened to you for a reason; there are no accidents. I shouldn't have punched that high school senior at the discotheque, but I am where I am today because of it.

Because of that punch, I went from Moldova to the United States, which truly was a dream when I was younger; it felt like it could never be reality.

I was given opportunities, and I took them whenever I could, from the English interview at university to meeting Gareth in Las Vegas. If I hadn't gone to that interview, I never would have come to the United States. If I had decided to go scuba diving for Thanksgiving instead of going to Las Vegas, I would have never met Gareth or been a part of Nutriband. Gareth would have sold his shares of the company, and he would not have had the control necessary to manufacture Nutriband patches. At the end of the day, I'm left with gratitude for where I find myself now.

That isn't to say there were no battles along the way. As you've seen, I've been tested and made many mistakes of my own, but I have held onto my morals in business.

I know that if I were to take the same routes that Vadim or Kalmar did, I would not be doing the right thing. Those shortcuts never pay off because they end up creating a lot of problems for you down the road. At the end of the day, you have to live with yourself. If I took those same shortcuts, I just know that wouldn't be me; I would be letting down not just myself, but my family and the people that are most dear to me.

If I faced these same deals again, I would approach them differently; I could have solved each one of my past deals with the knowledge I have now, and they would have been extremely successful. I just didn't know how to react at the time because I didn't have the experience or, as I later found out, the necessary life scars.

Now, I have had enough betrayal in my business deals to know that it is a painful experience, especially if it's someone you trust completely and unconditionally. When this happens, the first thing you want to do, no matter who they are, is give them another chance. My advice now would be not to do that; it can and will happen again. With business and in life, you need to be cautious all of the time and make sure you know who you are working or dealing with. You also have to be very lucky to meet the right people. Anybody who reaches even moderate success and denies that luck had anything to do with it is fooling themselves.

If I had trusted referrals, like I did with Gareth, I would have chosen entirely different business partners, but it's only with experience that I can share this wisdom. All of those experiences make you who you are, and good or bad, they will guide you down your own personal path. If you work past the hardships and mistakes, cherish the good and the wholesome, you can live a life with real happiness without regrets. It is because of my years on this earth that I made my first million that guided me to Mount Kilimanjaro. At the end of the day, you can look out from the top of the mountain, but the view can only be truly appreciated if it was you who climbed to the top.

Scaling the Mountain: A Reflection

Mount Kilimanjaro is the tallest mountain in Africa, standing at 5,895 meters (19,340 feet). At that height, it's snow-capped, and it is the largest free-standing mountain rise in the world.[1]

When we first arrived in Tanzania, we took the first three days to see the Ngorongoro and Manyara Safari. We knew, or to better say, we suspected that after those three days in paradise, observing lions, elephants, giraffes, and other animals, we would be facing the exact opposite. This would probably be the most physically challenging adventure of our lives. After the safari, we traveled to Arusha, where we would spend the last night before we would be transported to the Kilimanjaro Park gate the following morning.

Upon arrival, we were briefed by the expedition crew; my friends and I felt we were prepared for the journey ahead. I'd been training for the hike for months, with part of my preparation being jiu-jitsu wrestling, something I had not done since the COVID restrictions hit. We were well aware of the risks but still believed in our own abilities and determination. The crew walked us through the gravity of our trek: it would be cold and difficult to breathe, and we'd be utterly remote, so being transported off of the mountain by helicopter in an emergency would not be an option. Our route, the Lemosho Route, was the second hardest of the paths. We were to reach the summit on the sixth day and be back at the park's gates on the seventh day; we would reach the point of no return on the third day. Even still, I felt empowered, knowing what this trip stood for. It was an acknowledgement of myself and what I have been able to accomplish with my own two hands.

Safari

Maassai

In truth, the hike and climb were harder than we believed it would be; the thin air nearly brought us to our knees with altitude sickness. Had I not been in shape from judo and jiu jitsu, I could have seen myself being in real trouble making it to the summit. I had dreamed of taking my son with me on this trek sometime soon, but as a grown man in good shape, I struggled with it, and I knew my son wasn't ready for the mountain's intensity. We were scaling areas that were difficult even with the help from the expedition crew, hugging rocks as we scrambled up Barranco Wall. After all of my research on Kilimanjaro, it all felt familiar: to see a goal I very much wanted to reach and clearing obstacles every step of the way.

The mountain climb plans were made the night before engaging into the Kilimanjaro adventure.

The morning shadow, the whole day ahead.

We scaled the mountain in segments: we started the journey on Friday morning, and by Tuesday afternoon, we reached the last camp, Barafu Camp at 4,673 meters. We rested until 11 pm, had coffee and a small snack, and started the last climb to the summit at midnight. We needed to get to the summit by sunrise. Uhuru Peak was just five kilometers away, but this would be the toughest five kilometers we had ever traversed. We hiked for the next six hours through pitch black night, treading carefully as we ascended the final stretch of the mountain to reach Uhuru Peak.

For the first couple of hours, I was actually enjoying the walk, looking at the magnificent sky at times and making wishes on the falling stars, but after two hours, when we passed through the 5,000 meters altitude mark, it became extremely hard. It was a struggle just to breathe, particularly under the weight of my clothing. At times, it reminded me of the prep in my jiu-jitsu class, where I would have about two or three five-minute fights in a row, and then I would feel like vomiting and be short of breath, so I would skip the next fight and rest... Only, on the mountain, there was no skipping anything, there was no rest, and there were five more hours of constant fighting.

At times, the line between reality and dream faded as we pushed to put one foot in front of the other. At about 3 am, our water completely froze as we were facing about -15 centigrade temperatures and strong winds. Those last two hours before we reached Stella Point became a delirious blur. I was just constantly praying in silence, reciting "Our Father" in my mind, over and over again. I thought back to the dinner with Igor when we first heard the stories of climbing Kilimanjaro. I clearly recall the words "easy hike to the top" being said—there was nothing easy about it.

First light was just breaking when I took that final step and reached Stella Point. We were met with gale force winds and a loud, constant rumble that forced us to yell just to be able to hear each other. We cleared the ridge, and from that point, it was about another hour of walking to Uhuru Peak, the summit.

About 20 minutes into the walk to Uhuru peak, I stopped and fixed my GoPro to capture the sunrise. Then, it happened. The feeling is difficult to describe: I felt as if suddenly being charged with 1,000,000 volts, and tears were bursting from my eyes. I was hit with such an inflow of energy that I felt like I could jog from that point all the way to the summit.

Standing on the top of Kilimanjaro, it was a strange sight to behold: the little bit of mountain below us looked like an alien landscape full of craters and rocks, and the clouds covered the rest of the world, creating this island in the sky. As the orange sun tinged the final limits of the horizon, giving way to the blue sky, I wondered how I had ended up at the very limits of Tanzania. From a small town in Moldova to the highest point in Africa, I was reminded of how far I had come despite all of the odds against me; I will never forget that moment of triumph. It was humbling to see everything I had accomplished and the world stretched out in front of my feet.

We paused atop the mountain for each of us to reflect on our journey, appreciate the view, and of course, take photos. We brought with us a Moldovan flag and a flag with Nutriband's logo; it felt important to bring these keepsakes with us all the way to the top. They didn't add much weight to our packs, but they represented so much. It was especially important for me to present the Nutriband flag as it is a true reminder for me of what can be accomplished in the face of adversity if you have the right people by your side. I thought back to my parents, who always supported my education; my beautiful wife Jazmina, who encouraged all of my business ventures; and my two children, who are the light of my life and my proudest accomplishments. I couldn't wait to see my family and share all that I felt and saw atop the mountain. While I was recording the view from the summit with my GoPro, I heard myself thinking aloud, "So, this is how it feels to be on top of the world…"

On our way down, it was not a quick descent. After four hours, we reached the camp that we had left from at midnight. Once we ate a quick lunch, we had to descend to an altitude of 3,200 meters to the last camp. By the end of this seven hour leg of the descent, we felt pain in every step. This only worsened our altitude sickness, getting to the point of not being able to keep food down for one of my friends. The frequent stops meant we would not make it to the camp before sunset. We were there to help each other, encouraging one another to keep moving forward down the trail.

We arrived at our last camping site after it was already dark. We were completely exhausted. One of my friends crashed in his tent right away. My other friend and I made an attempt to have some soup that was prepared for us, but after a couple of sips, we just went back to our tents and followed suit. The mattress and the sleeping bag felt softer and more comfortable than at any time during that trip. We woke up with bird sounds, another thing that we did not hear for the last four days; we were in the cloud forests of Kilimanjaro. When we awoke, we felt rejuvenated, and the next 10 kilometers to the Kilimanjaro National Park gate, even under the pouring rain, felt like just another "walk in the park." We arrived at our Arusha Hotel on Thursday afternoon, and that same night, we flew to Istanbul.

In Istanbul, Turkey, I completed another item on my bucket list: I visited Hagia Sophia, built originally by the Roman Emperor Justinian I. I recovered from the trip and caught up on the world before I boarded a plane back to the US three days later.

I set out to Kilimanjaro dismayed that I could not bring my children along on this journey. To see my son hiking alongside me would have been an ultimate joy, but I soon realized that this was not the hike for him yet. I believe that this hike to Kilimanjaro's summit was meant for my own personal reflection; a certain strength and experience was necessary for me to see that I have reached a point in my life where I can stand tall and feel pride in all that I have achieved.

Now, having returned from Tanzania, there is the question of "What next?" It is not an easy question to answer because the future is inherently unknown; also, I have not put my next goal in place to reach for. I am not looking to put another number down that I will be able to point to and signal another mountain to climb.

Instead, I have something now that the younger version of myself would have been dreaming about: a family with a beautiful wife and two children. If I am looking for the next mountain, it has to be one we can all climb together; otherwise, it will not hold any meaning for me.

To have been able to climb Kilimanjaro, long after making my first million dollars and before I turned 50, signifies an enduring life lesson for us all: you can achieve the seemingly impossible, one step at a time. My time with my family will only grow more precious, in the same way that my memories of my family in Moldova are invaluable. I now know better than to take life for granted as I have now seen the sunrise over Kilimanjaro.

A 27 year journey. There were still 5 days to go from this point.

This is how it feels - on top of the world.

Uhuru Peak, 5895 meters (19341 Ft.), with Vitalie Avram (left) si Vitalie Blatnoi (right), my longtime friends that joined me on this epic adventure

Nutriband Inc. the main reason this dream became reality.

Vitalie Avram and I with the Moldovan Flag,
so we never forget the roots of where we came from.

The most beautiful sunrise in the world,

References

"Kilimanjaro." *National Geographic*. Last updated May 20, 2022. https://education.nationalgeographic.org/resource/kilimanjaro.

Bio

Serguei Melnik is an accomplished entrepreneur, linguist, and world traveler. From the villages of Moldova, Serguei used his work ethic and passion for business to chase his dreams in the US. Obstacles and red tape have only fueled Serguei's grit and determination to see his work through to success. He builds companies up and restructures them for profitable and sustainable growth.

From his early success in getting credit for listing the first Moldovan company to the American Stock Exchange and ringing the market opening bell in 2003 to the latest successful listing of Nutriband, Inc. on NASDAQ, Serguei has guided the initiation of trading multiple companies to the over-the-counter markets in the U.S., and has provided general advice with respect to the U.S. financial markets for companies located in the U.S. and abroad.

Serguei is currently the President and the Chairman of the Board of Directors of Nutriband, Inc., a company dedicated to the development of a portfolio of transdermal pharmaceutical products to provide relief and care to chronic pain patients. He co-founded the company with Gareth Sheridan in 2016 and successfully completed the IPO with simultaneous listing.

In addition to his career successes, Serguei has hiked mountains throughout the world, including Mount Kilimanjaro in Summer 2022. His proudest accomplishment, however, is the family he created with wife Jazmina, and their two kids.

Book Description

Entrepreneurialism is an uphill—or mountainous—battle filled with new challenges every day. Having come from Moldova's early days of democracy, Serguei Melnik has always thrived on adversity, studying hard and chasing opportunities. While in law school, Serguei made a promise that he would hike Mount Kilimanjaro with his friend when they'd earned $1 million.

That mountain became a symbol for every challenge Serguei would face, from fraudulent company partners to arriving poor in the US to the challenge of growing his family. Through all of these trials and successes, Serguei held tight to his integrity and followed his intuition to achieve personal and professional success. Serguei demonstrates that a person can not just survive, but thrive if they hold tight to their values and push through personal and professional roadblocks to enjoy the rewards at the finish line.

You can follow the verses of Vladimir Vysotsky in "Song About a Friend." Climbing to the business pinnacle is the same as climbing to the mountain summit: the true colors of your companion can and will come through:

> *"If he didn't complain or whine*
> *Clenching teeth through entire climb*
> *When you suddenly slipped and fell*
> *His hands fought with the rope but held*

If he acted as if at war
At the summit he swayed with awe
Doesn't matter what he might seem
You can place all your trust in him."

www.ingramcontent.com/pod-product-compliance
Lightning Source LLC
Chambersburg PA
CBHW051006140626
46546CB00016B/880